This Book Belongs to:

....

Writing Space

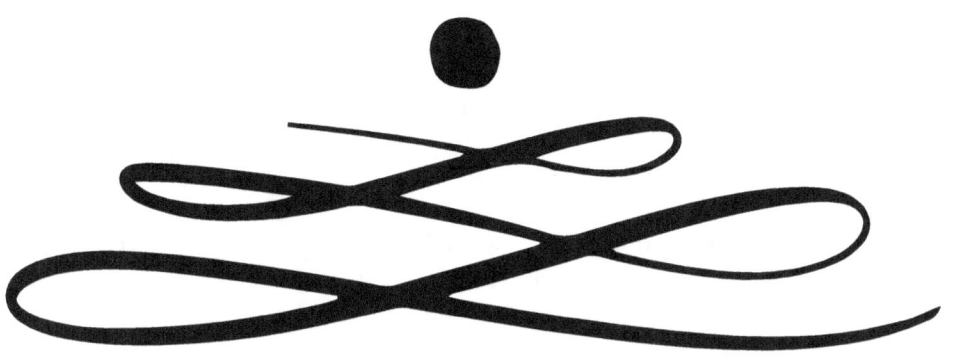

"When you rise in the morning, give thanks for the light, for your life, for your strength..."

- Tecumseh

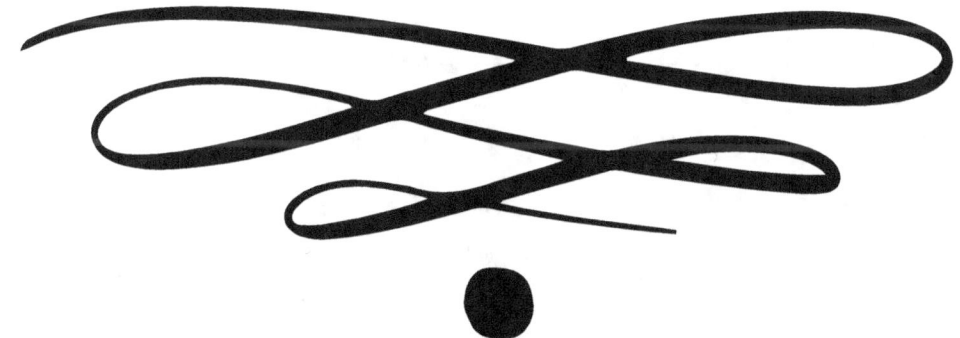

Writing Space

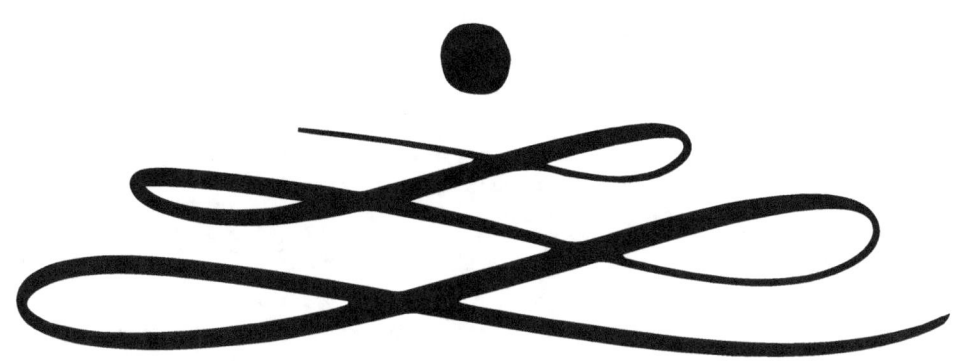

Write about a time you almost gave up.

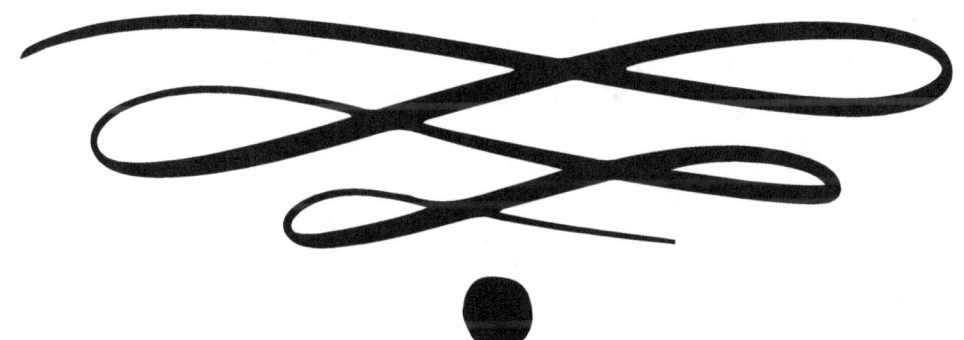

Writing Space

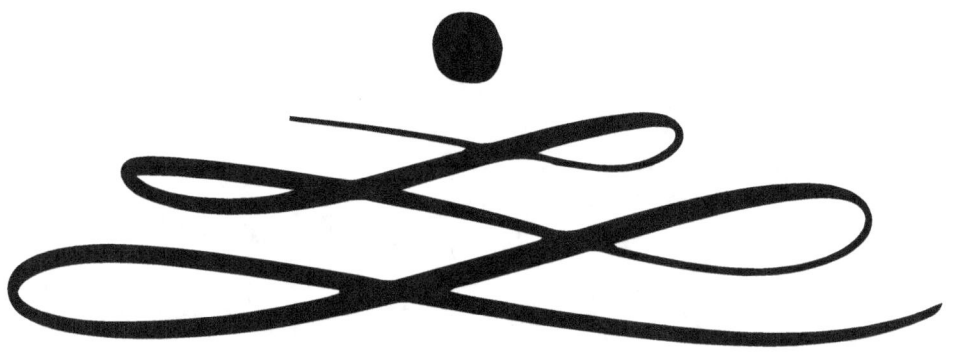

"The secret of getting ahead is getting started."

- Mark Twain, American writer and humorist, 1835-1910

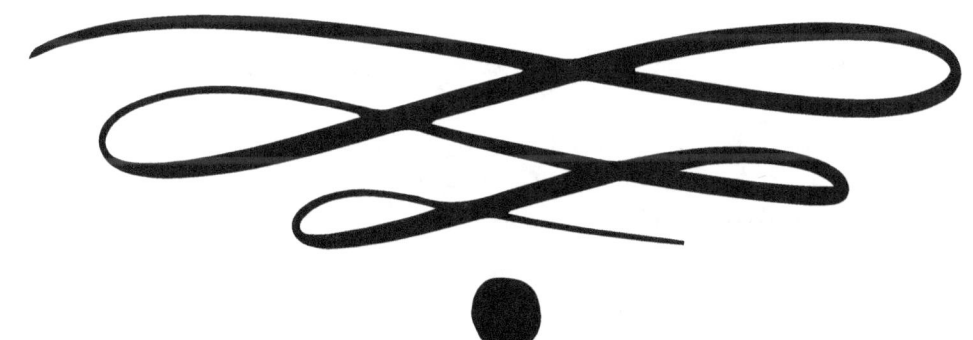

Writing Space

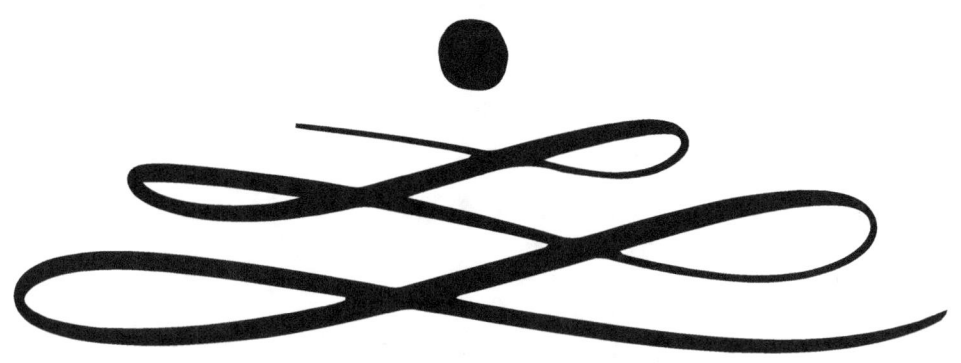

Write about your best moment yet.

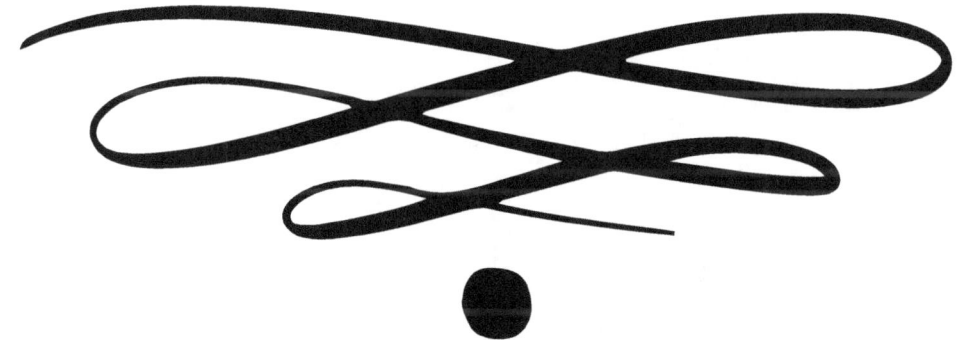

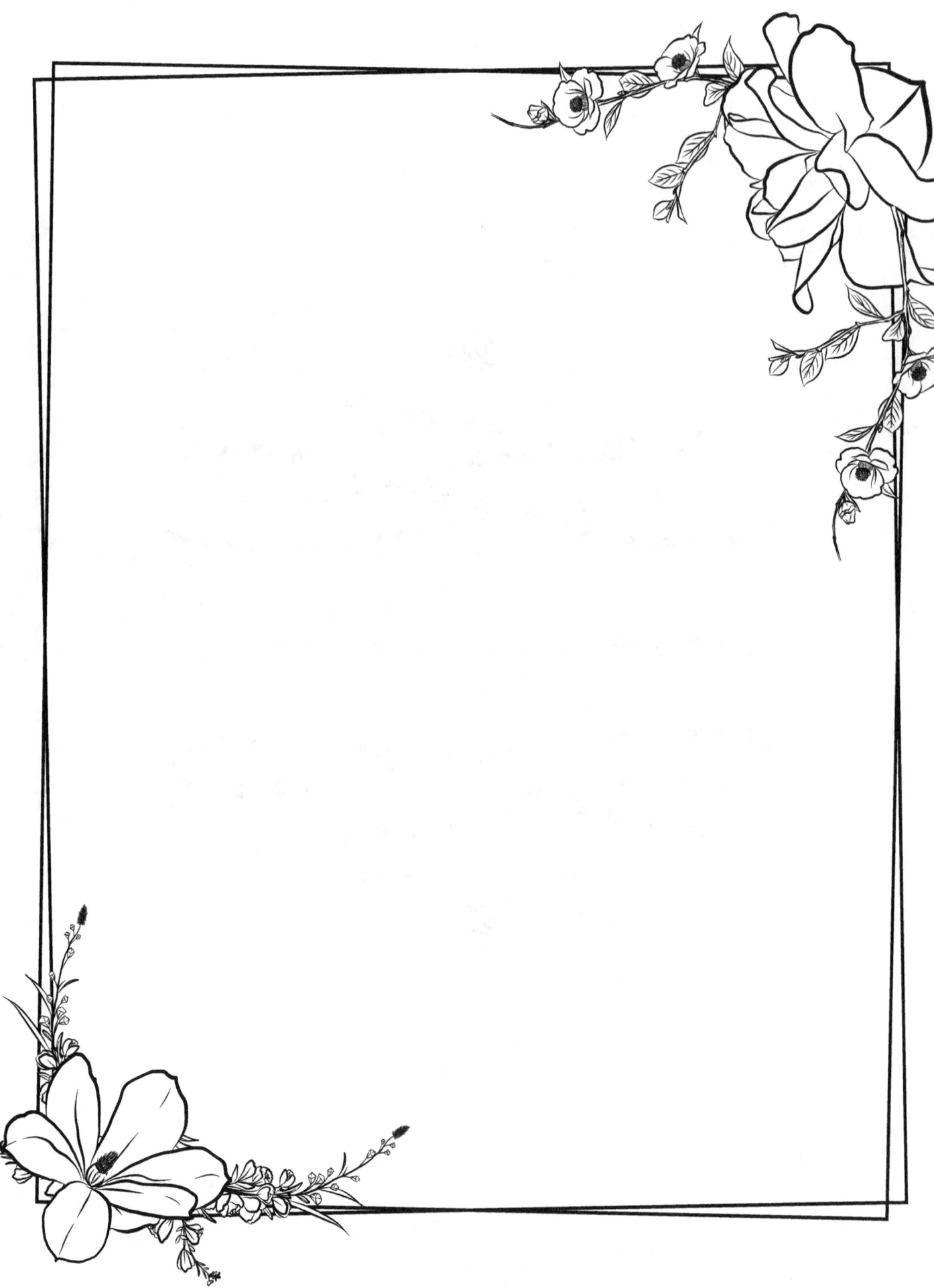

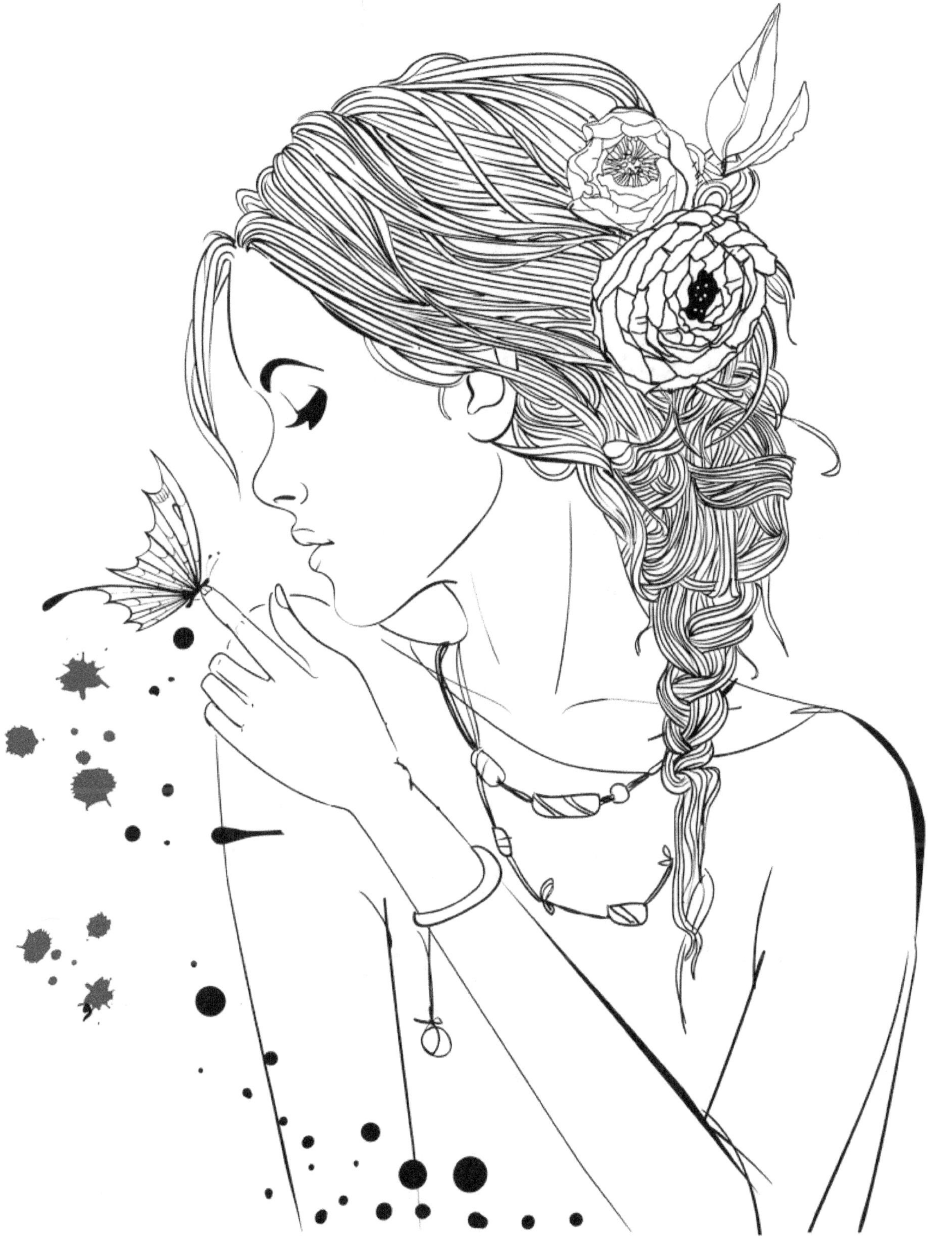

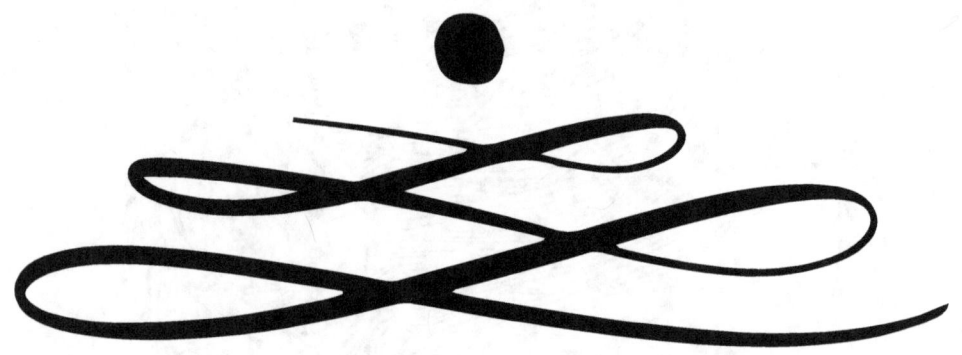

"Knowing is not enough; we must apply. Willing is not enough; we must do."

- Johann Wolfgang von Goethe, German writer and statesman, 1749-1832

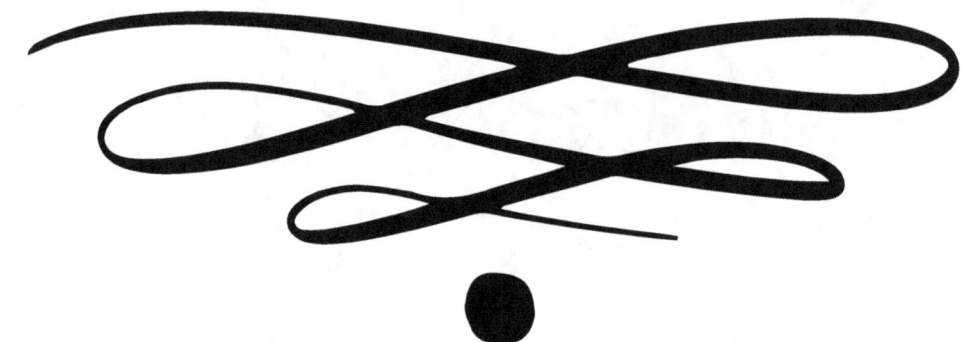

Writing Space

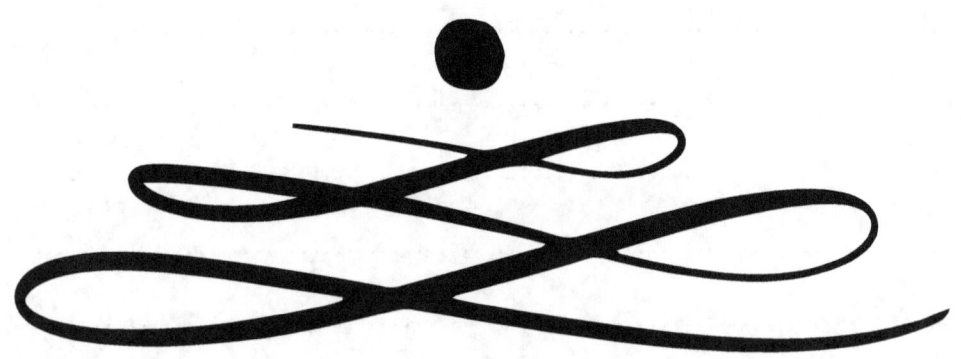

Write about a time you had a premonition.

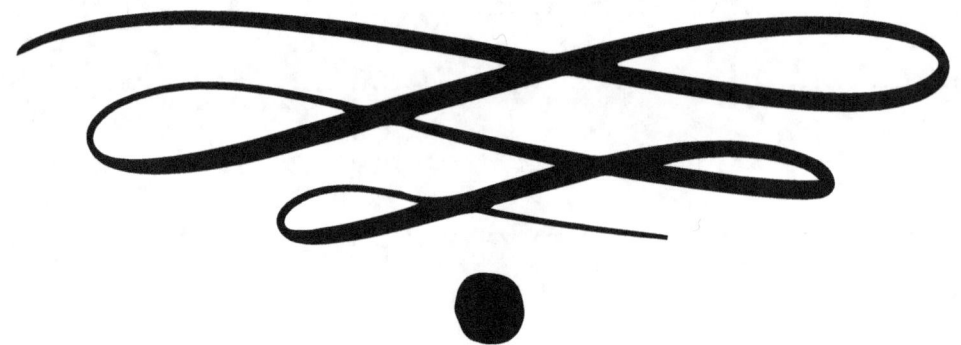

Writing Space

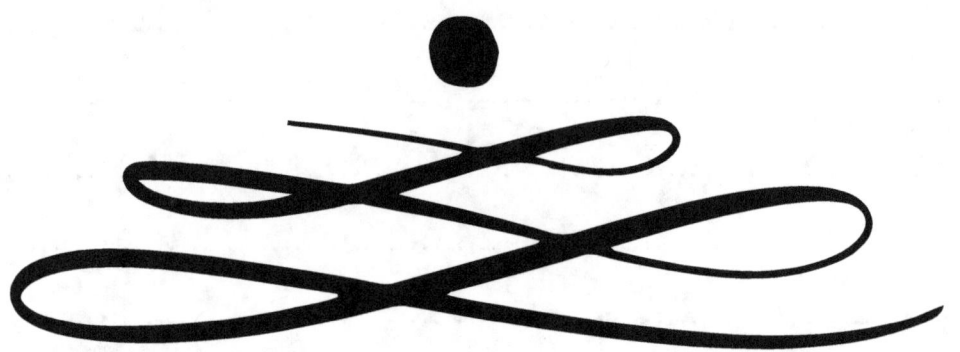

"Do not dwell in the past, do not dream of the future, concentrate the mind on the present moment."

- Gautama Buddha

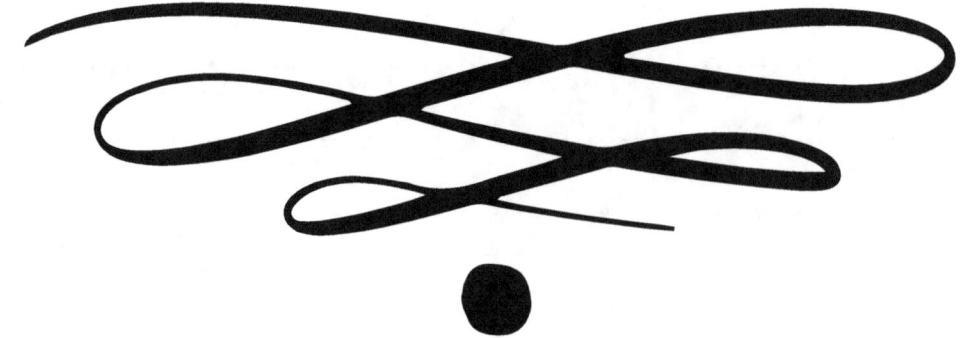

Writing Space

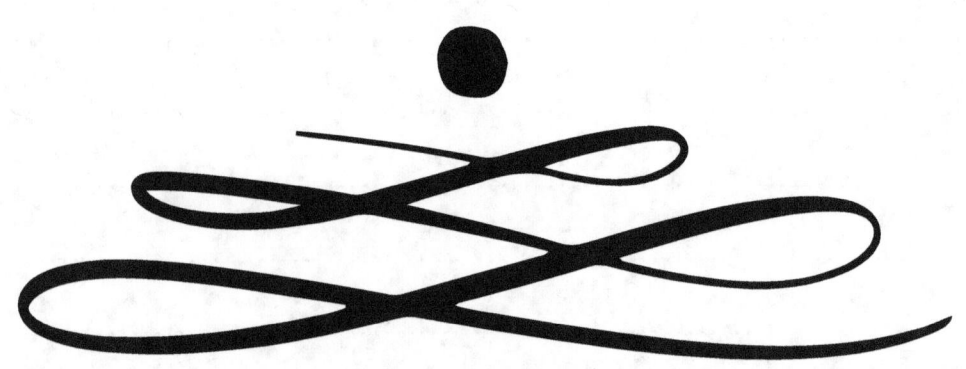

Write a poem about sadness.

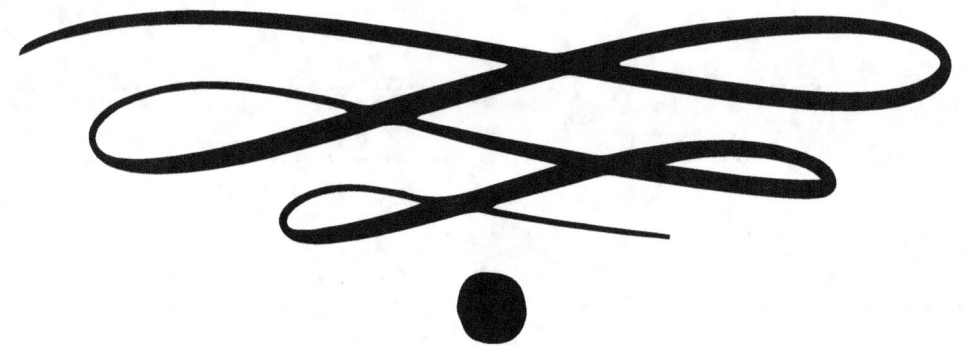

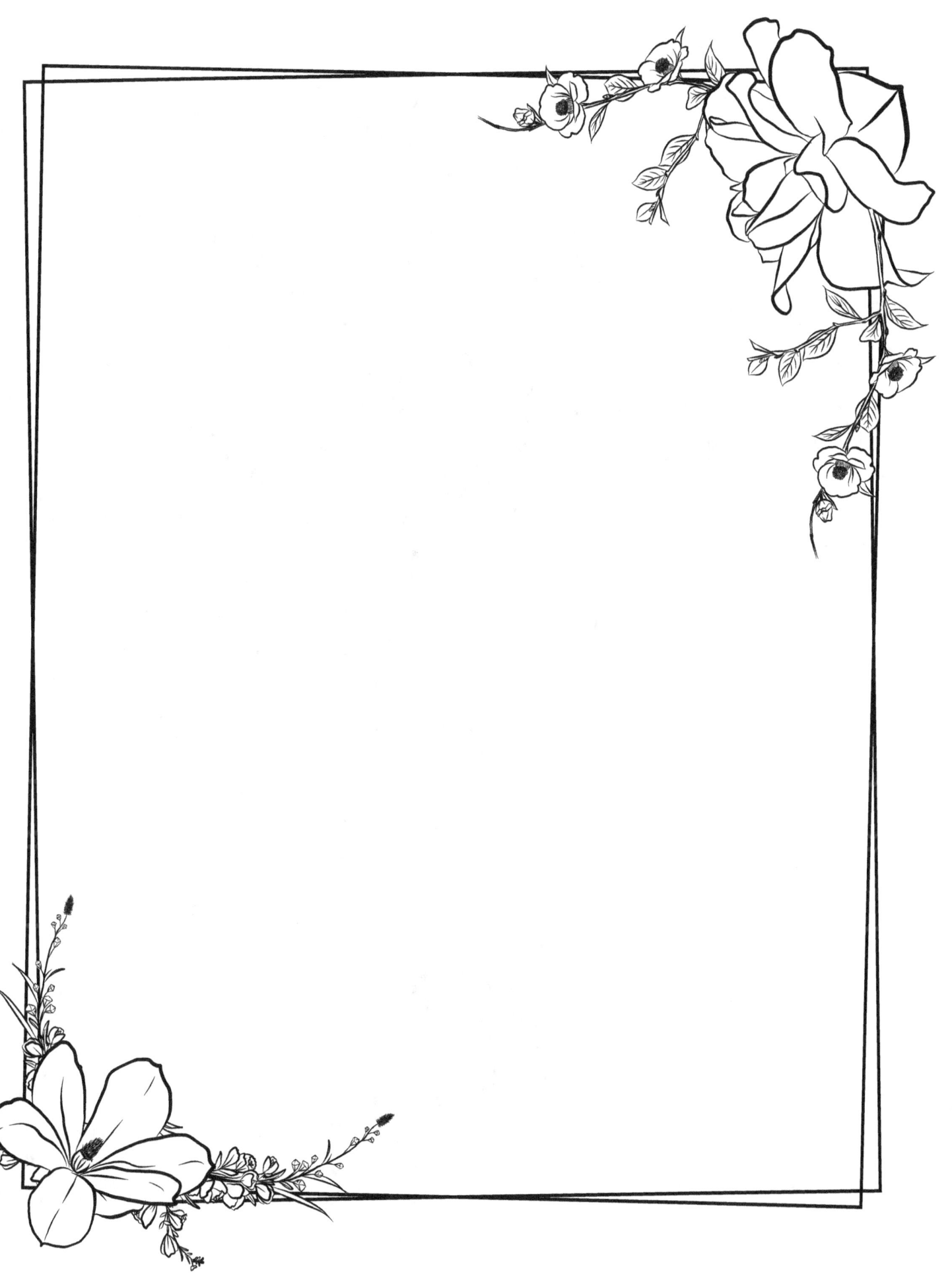

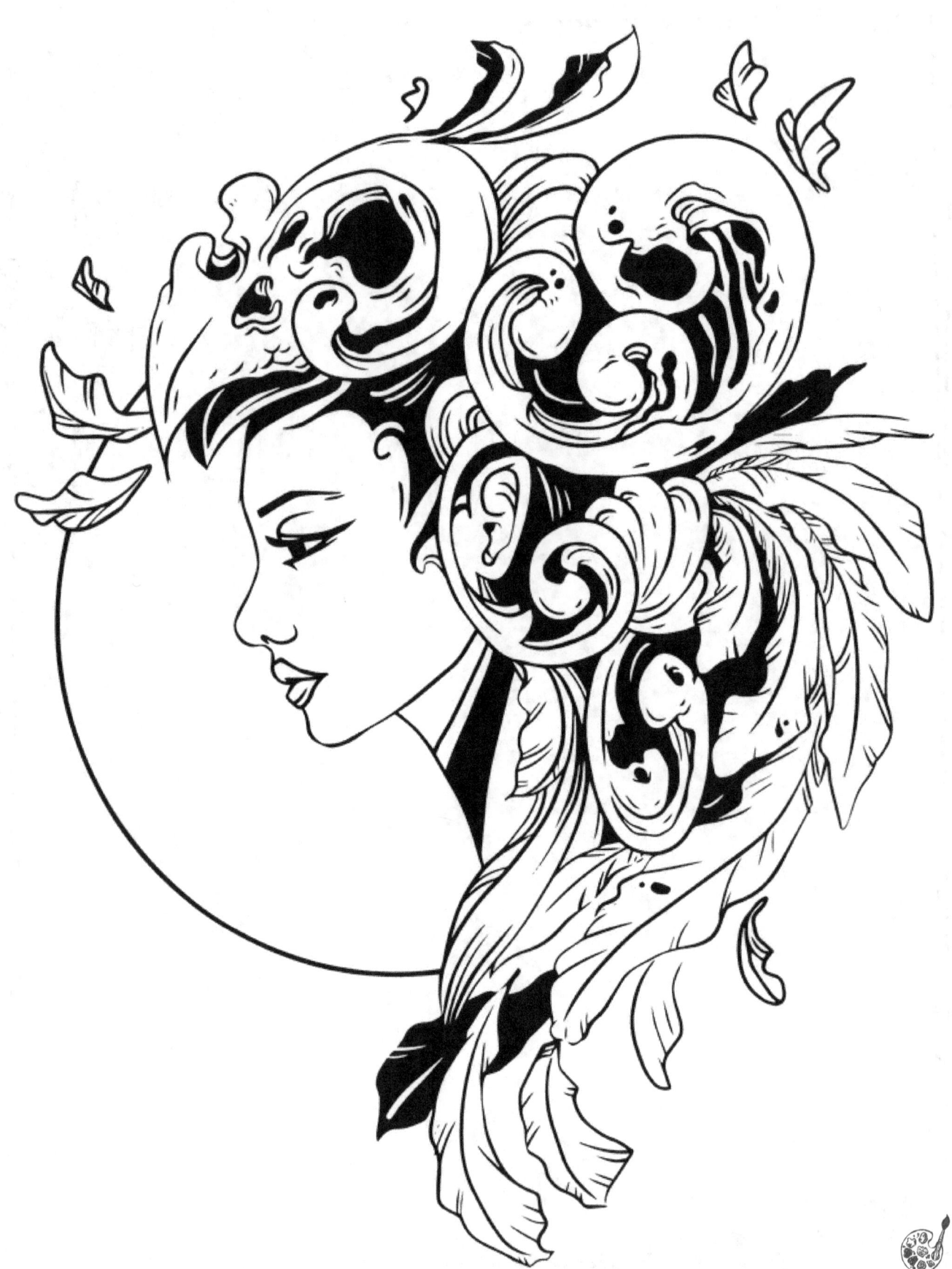

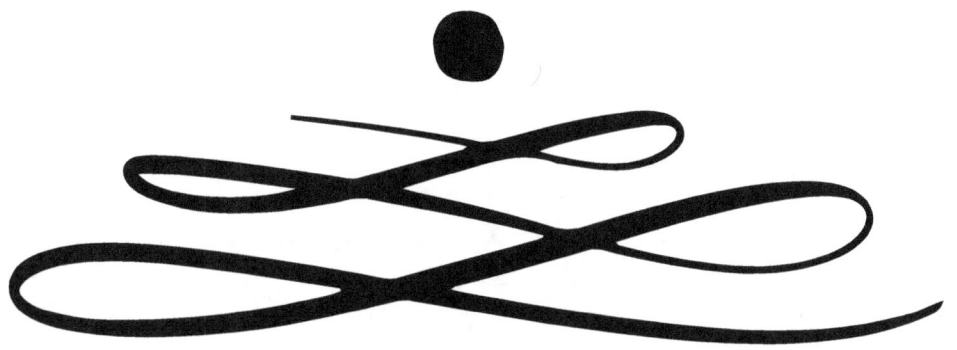

"The mind is everything. What you think, you become."

- Gautama Buddha

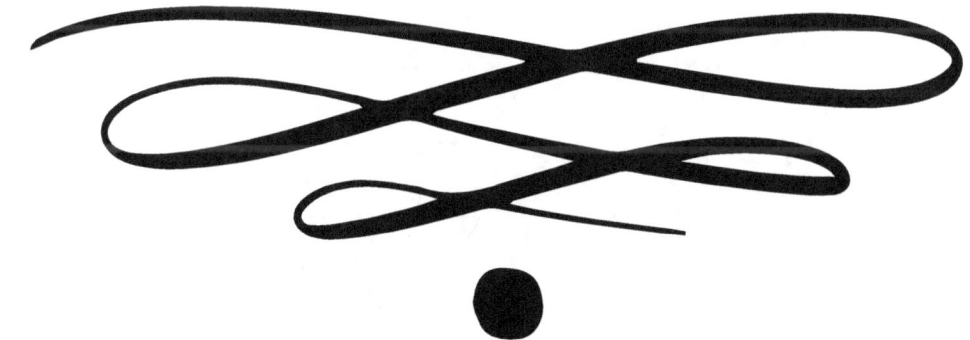

Writing Space

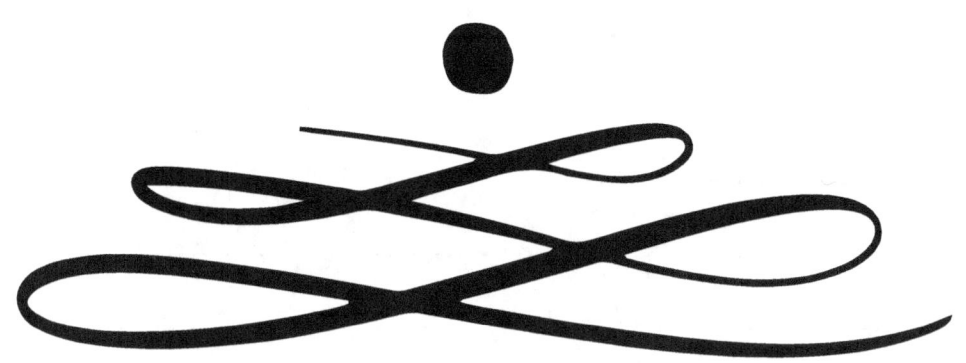

Write about reconciliation.

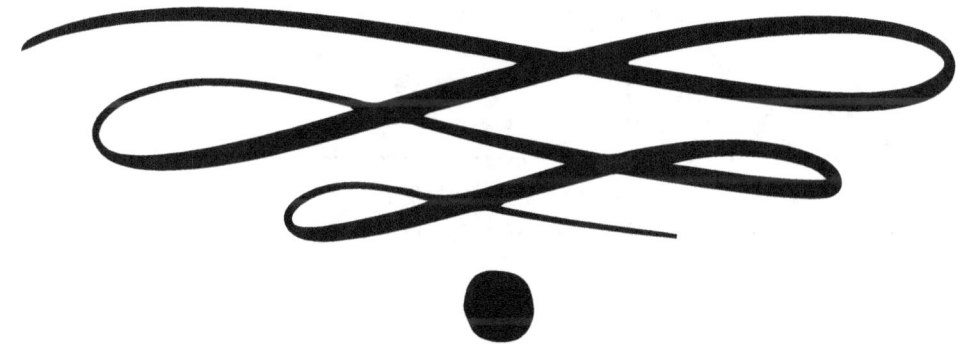

Writing Space

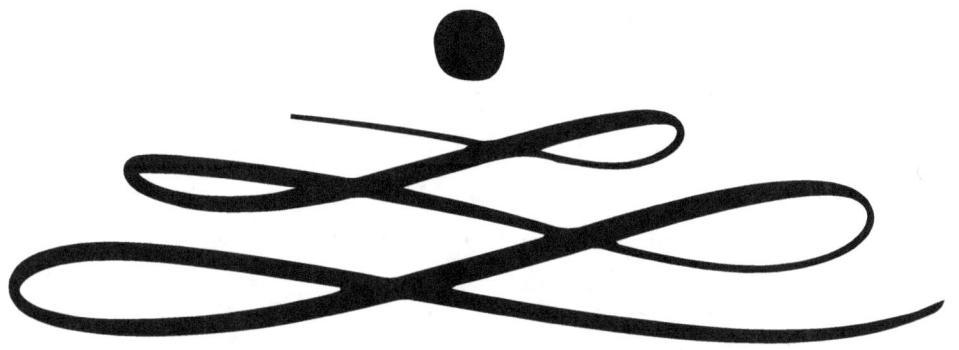

"The secret of getting ahead is getting started..."

- Mark Twain

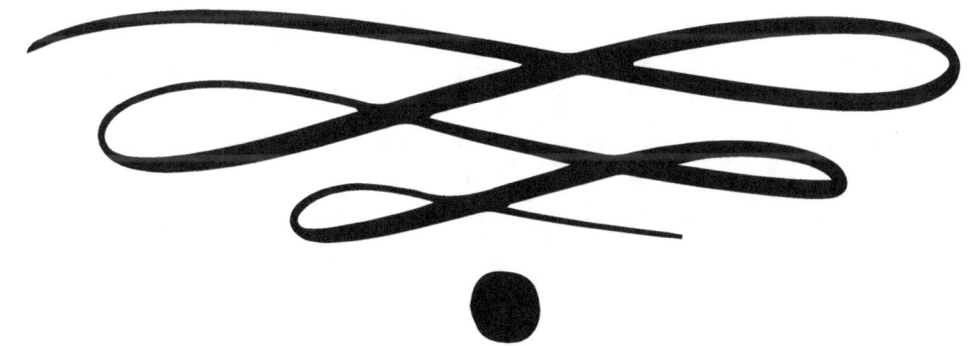

Writing Space

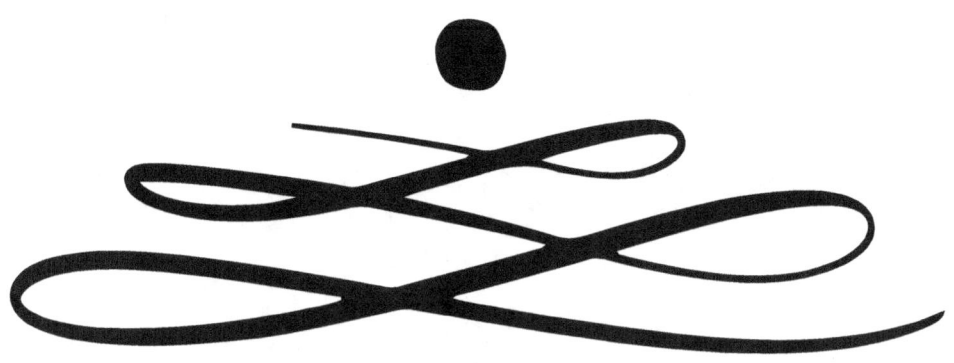

Write about a time when a stranger became a friend.

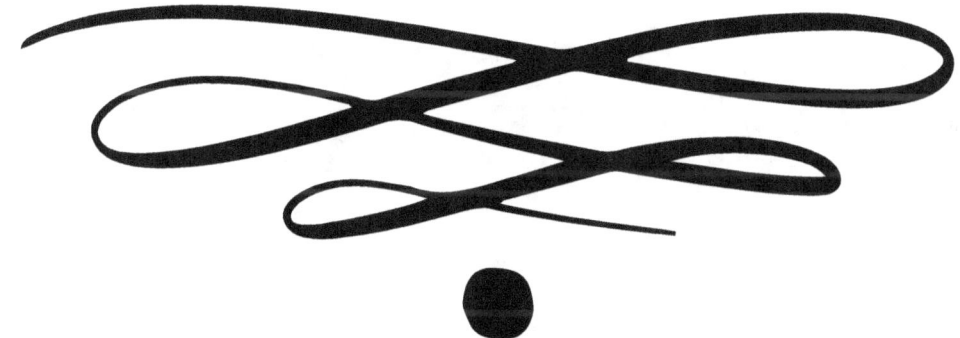

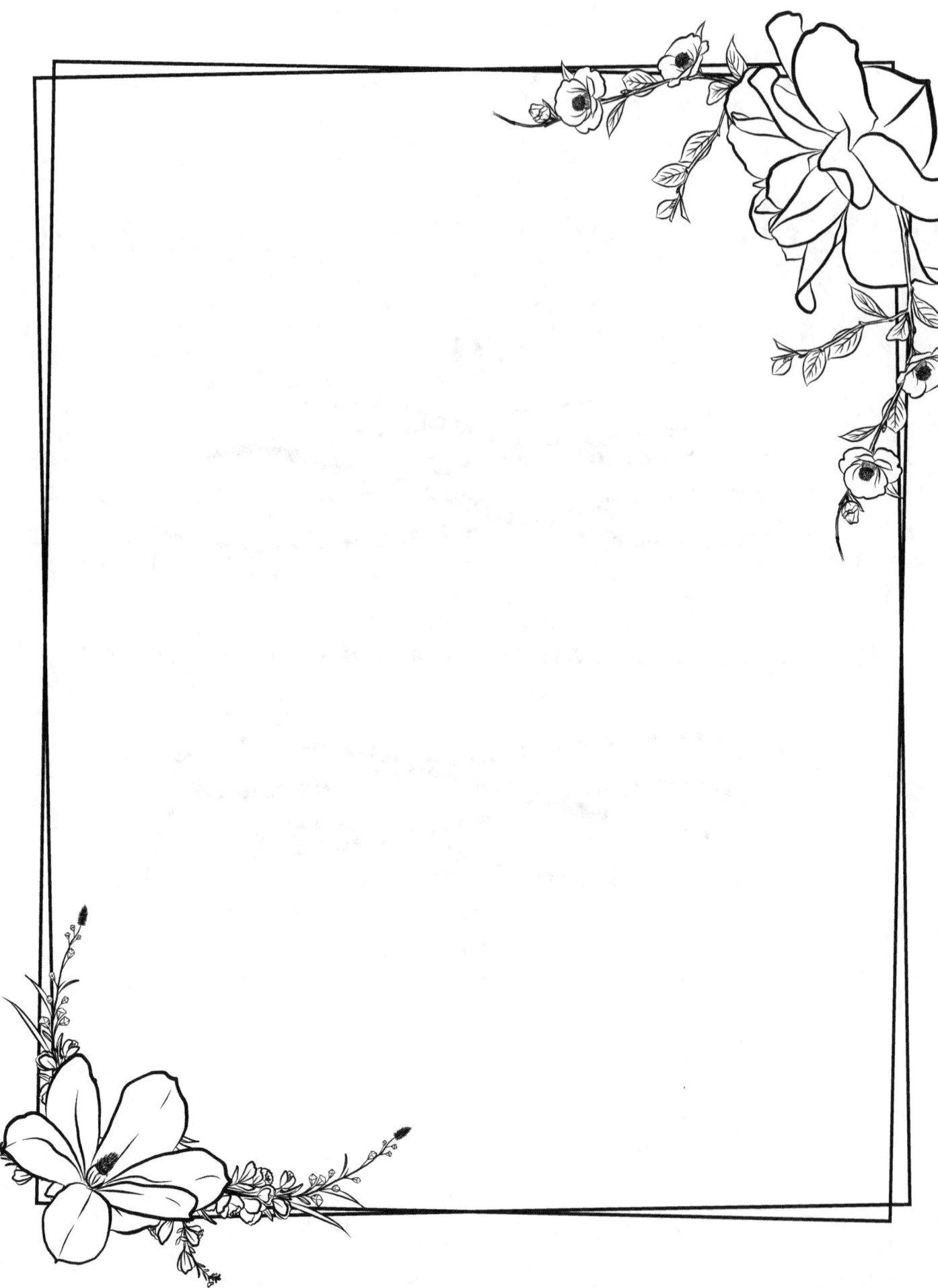

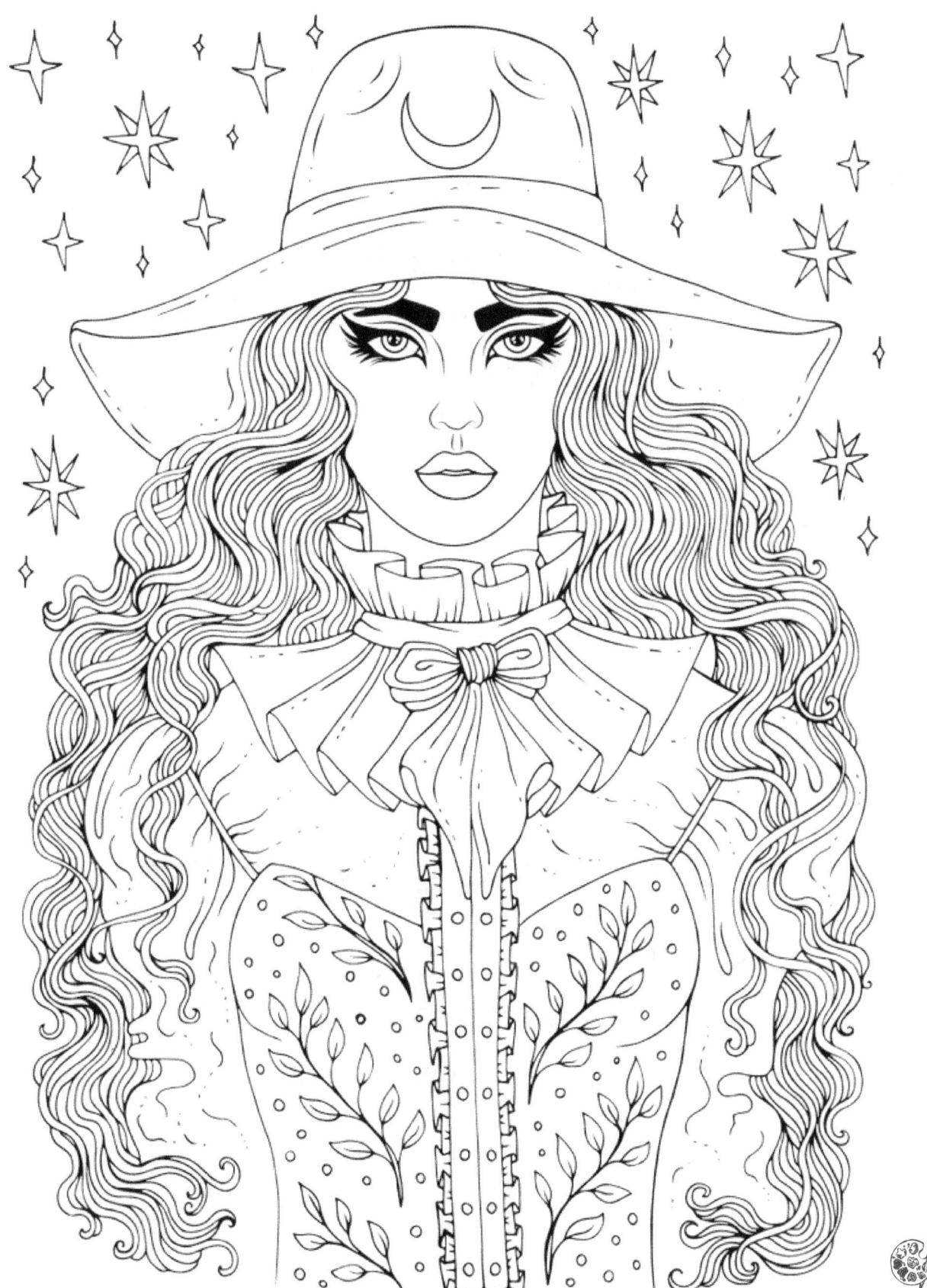

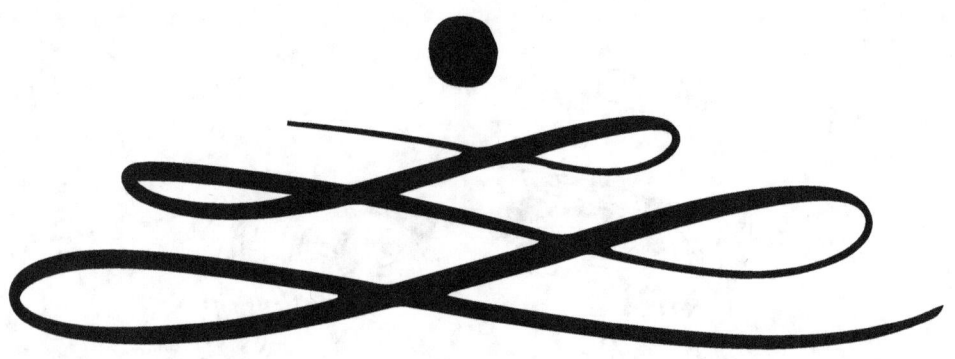

"We are shaped by our thoughts; we become what we think."

- Gautama Buddha

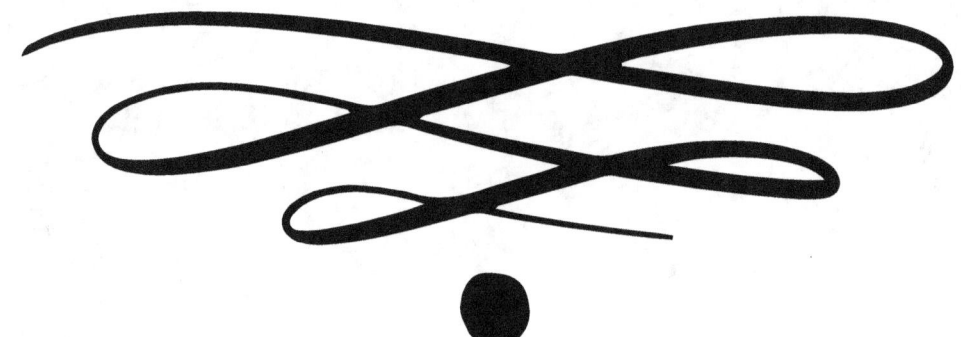

Writing Space

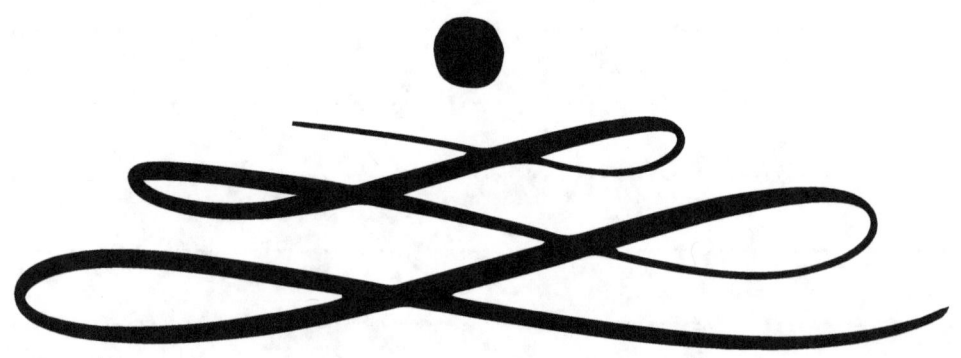

Write about the happiest moment of your childhood.

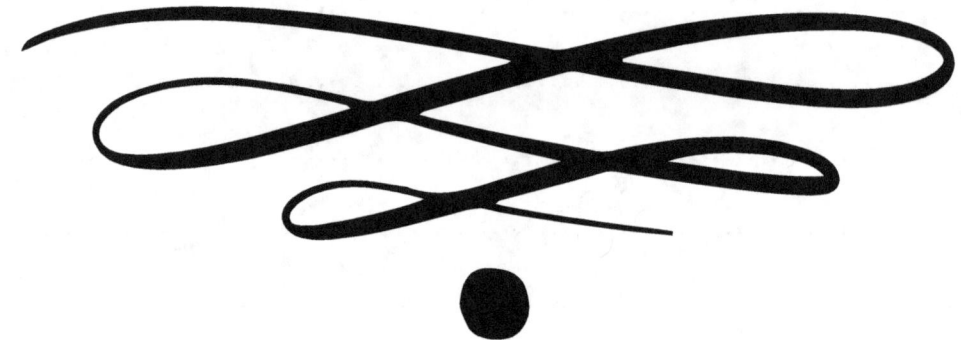

Writing Space

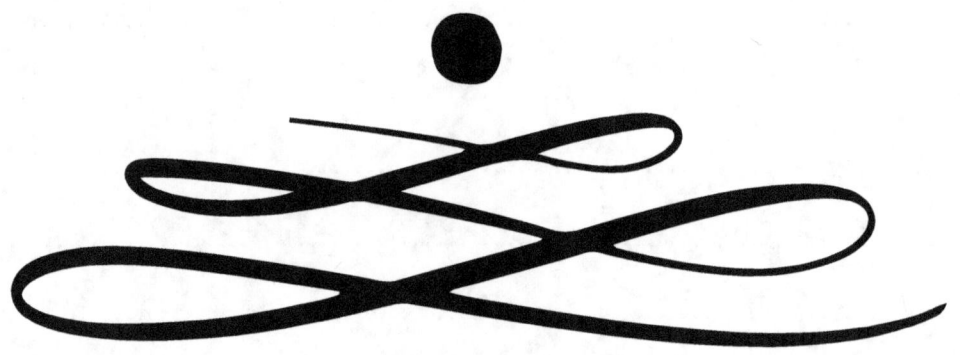

"Love inspires, illuminates, designates and leads the way..."

- Mary Baker Eddy

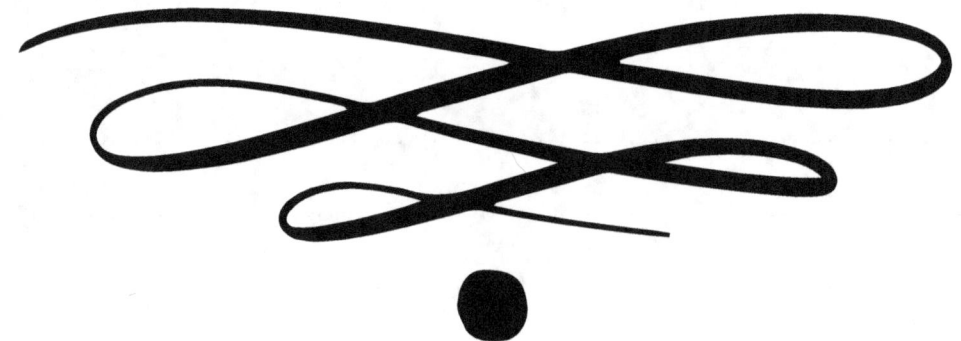

Writing Space

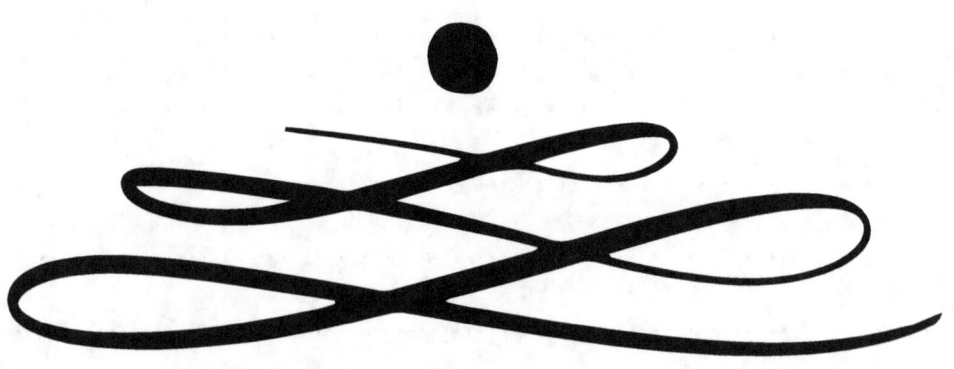

Imagine you had an interview with a character that you hated from your favorite book.

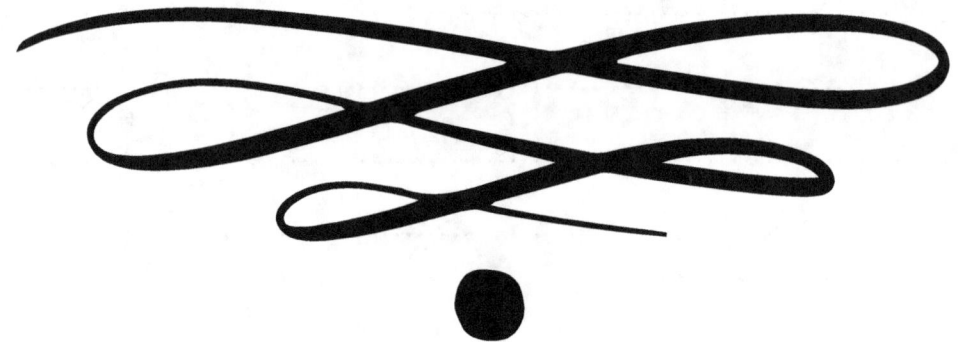

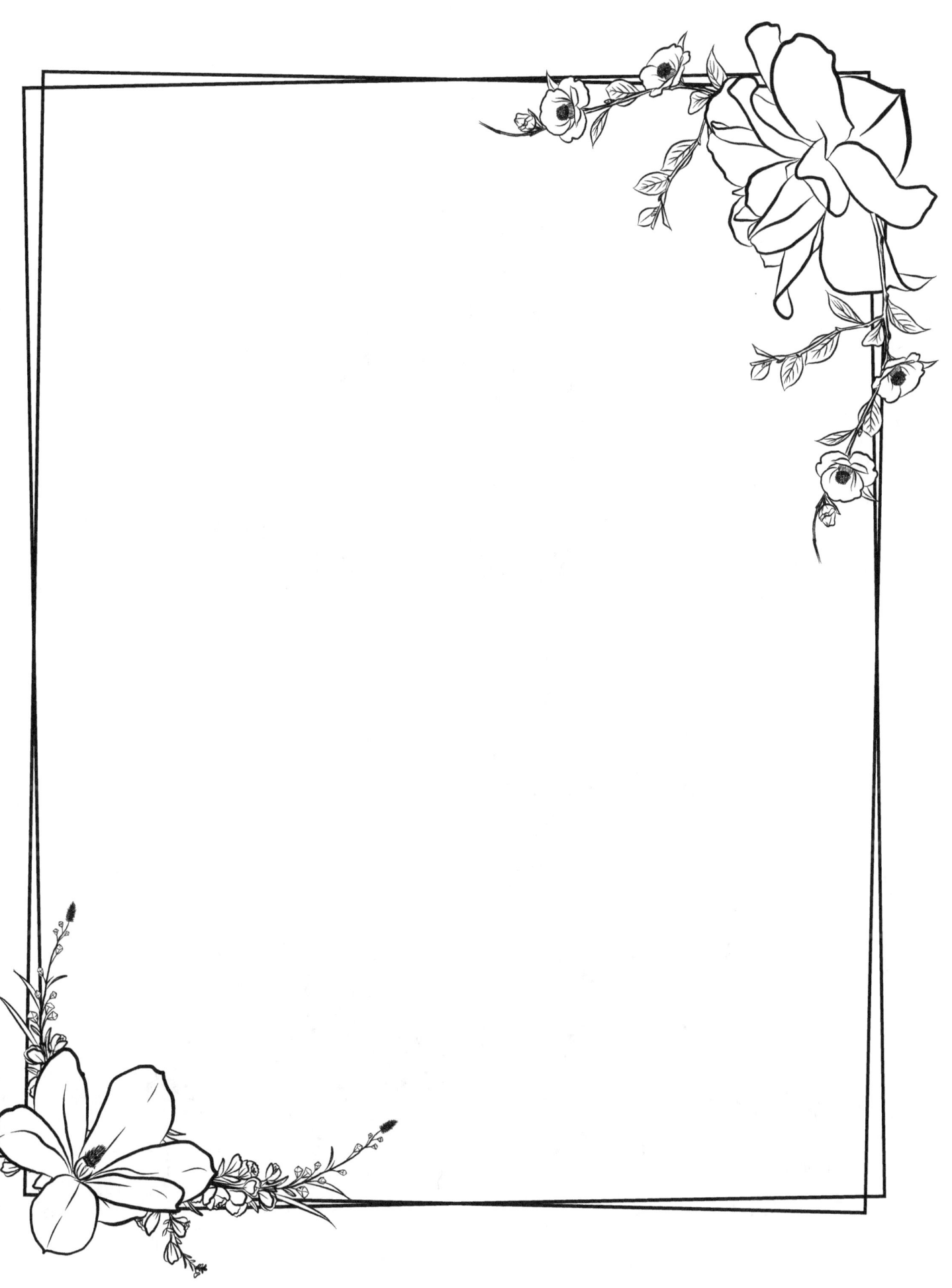

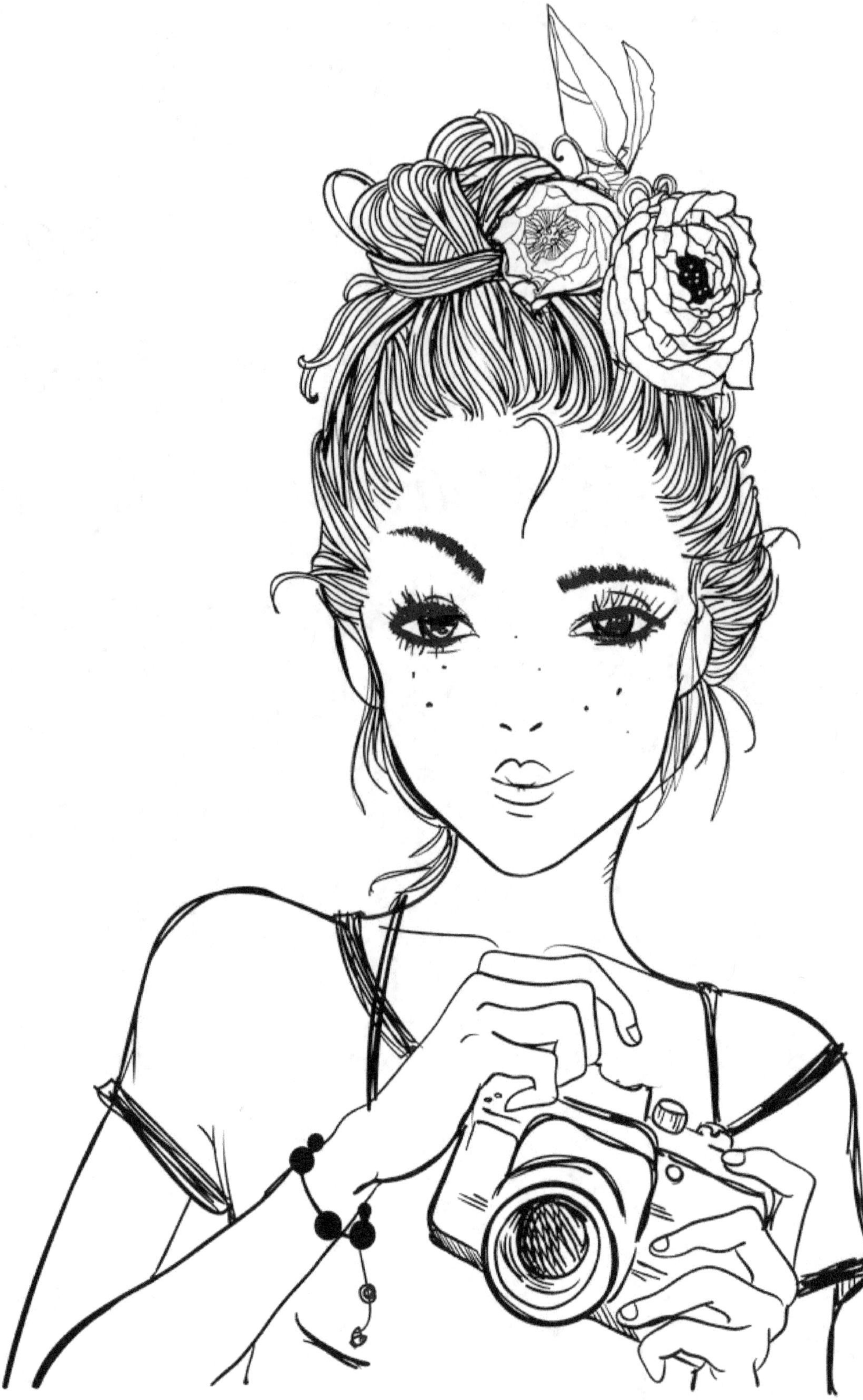

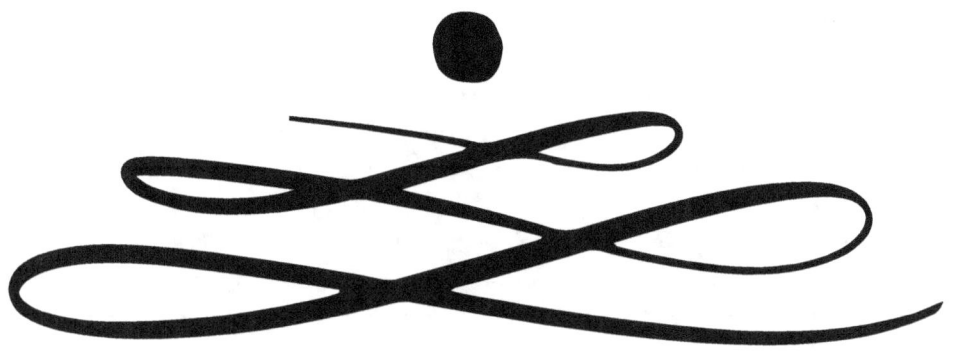

"I am not afraid; I was born to do this..."

- Joan of Arc

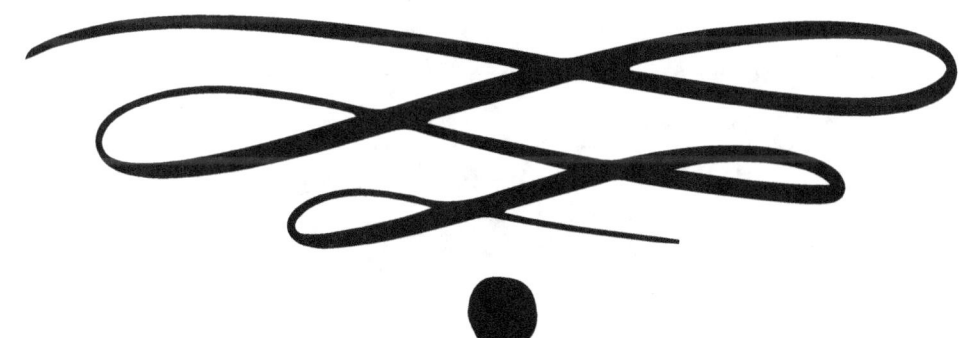

Writing Space

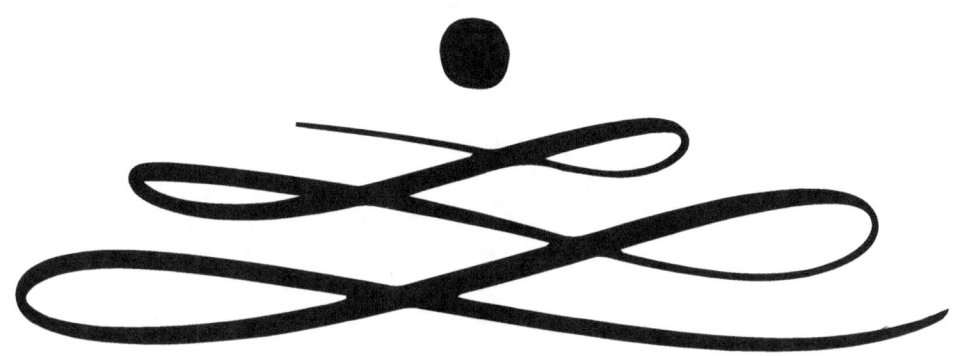

Write about the moment you fell in love.

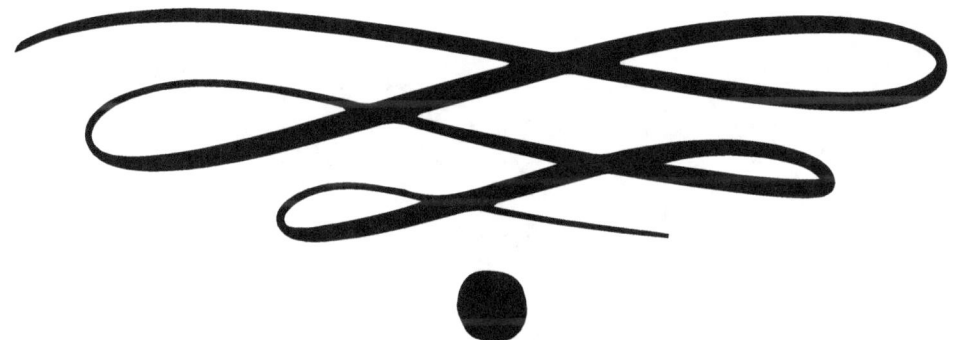

Writing Space

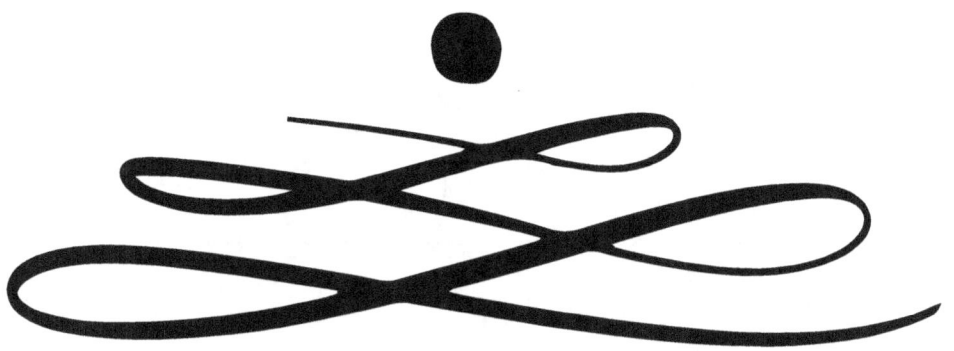

"Life is the flower for which love is the honey..."

- Victor Hugo

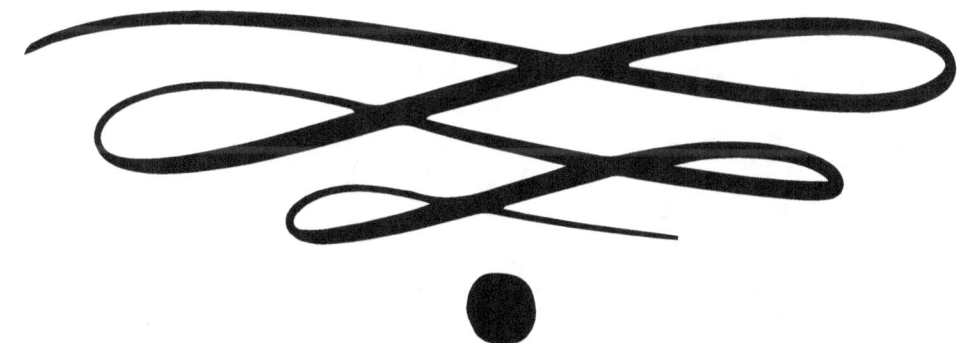

Writing Space

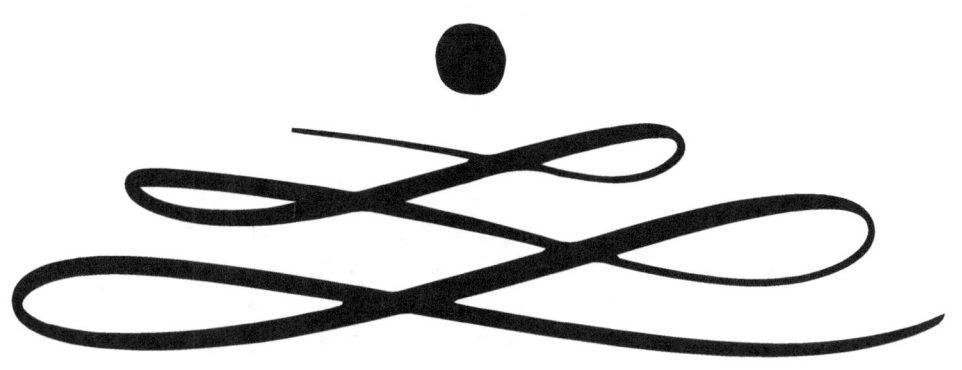

Imagine you ran into your old self at a bookstore. What would you say?

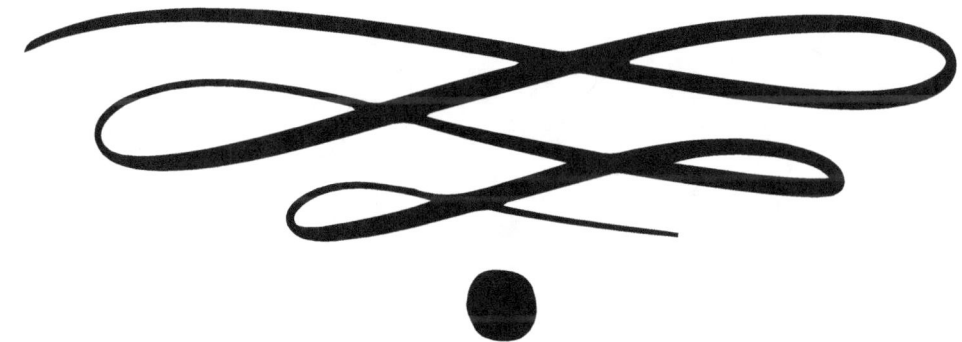

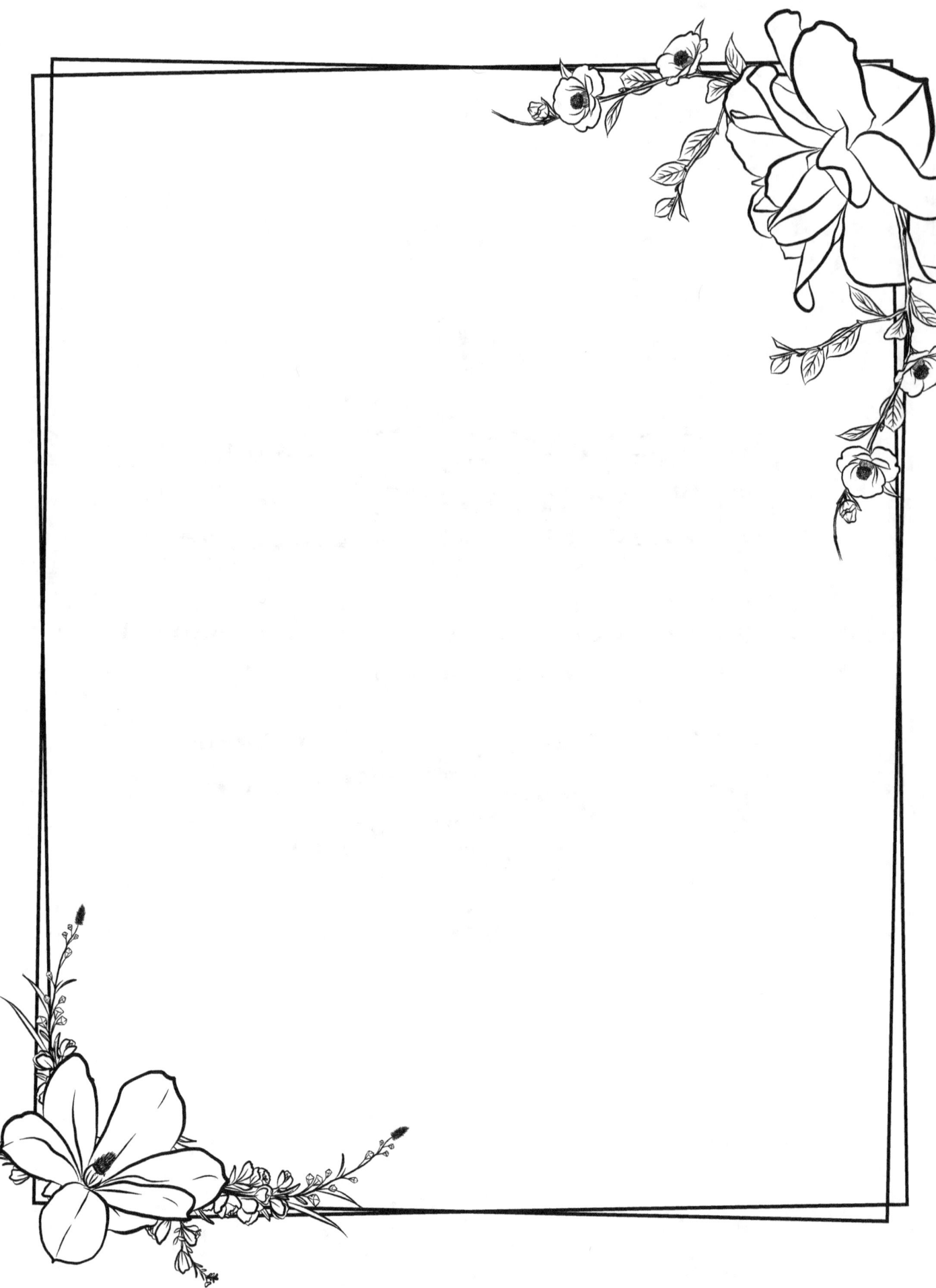

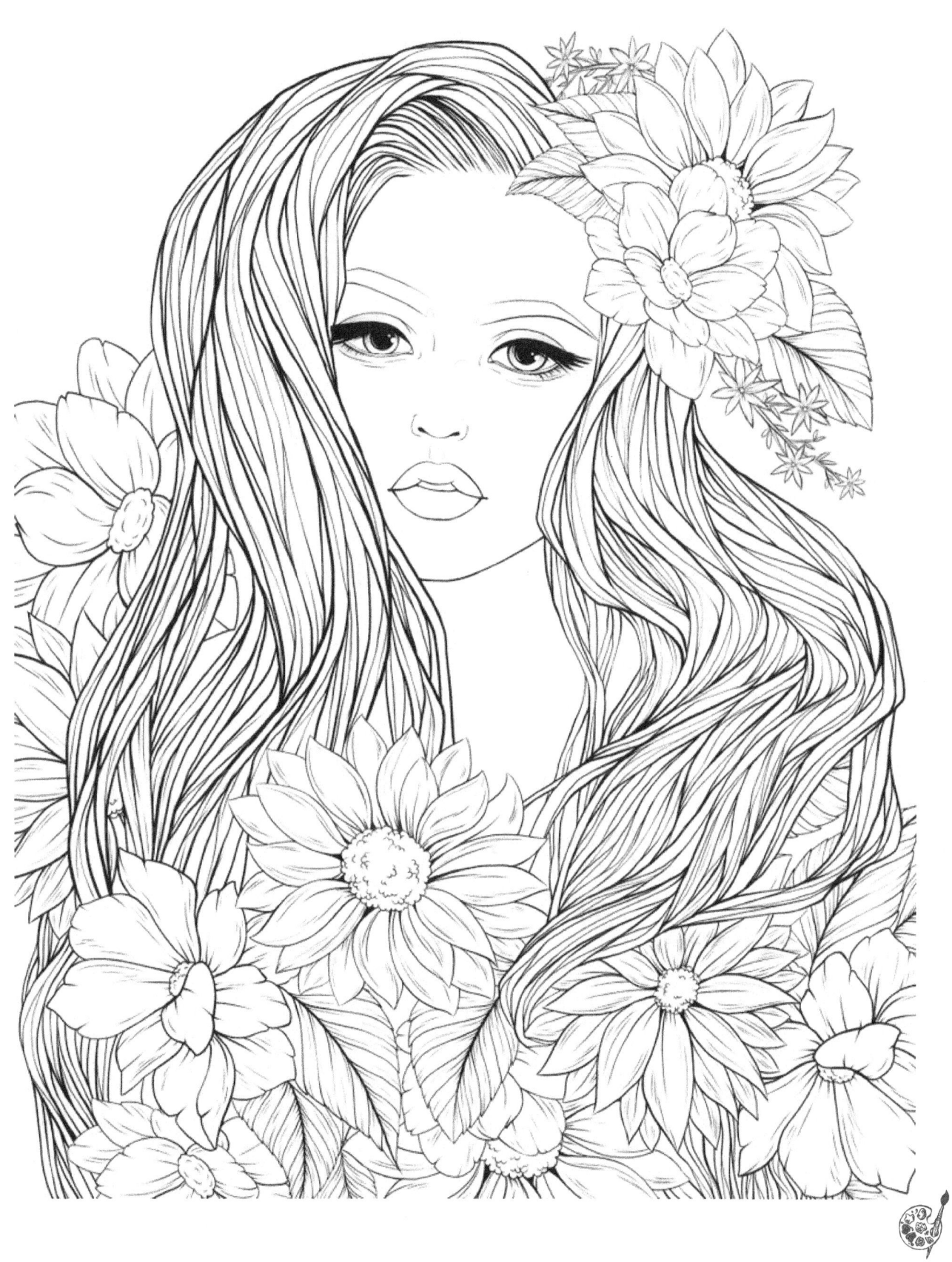

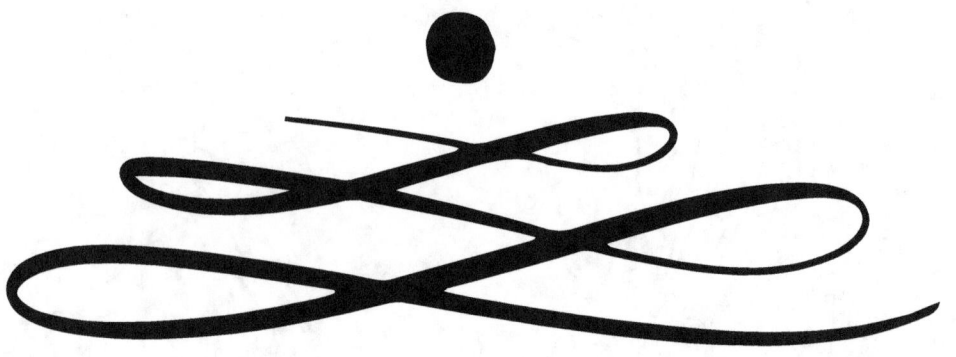

"For success, attitude is equally as important as ability."

- Walter Scott, Scottish novelist and poet, 1771-1832

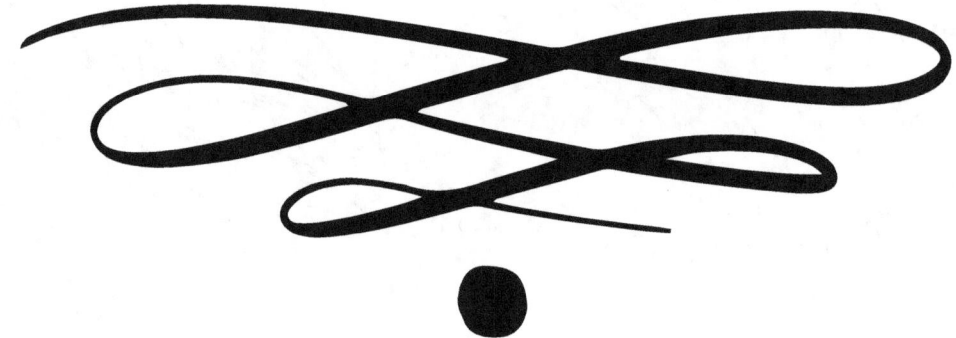

Writing Space

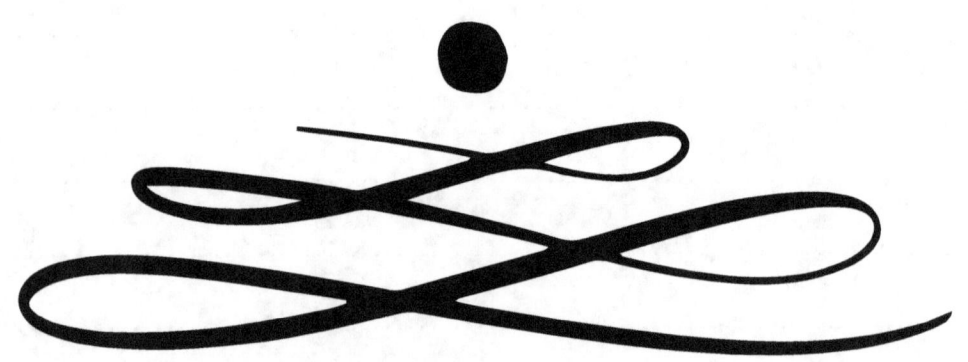

Are you very different from what you were five years ago? Why?

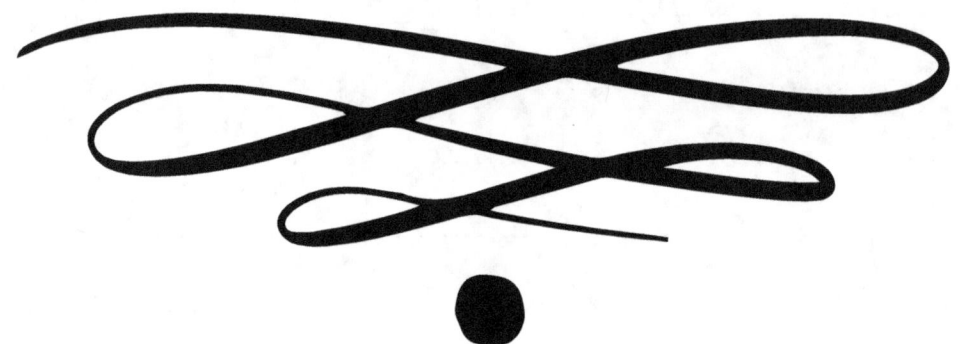

Writing Space

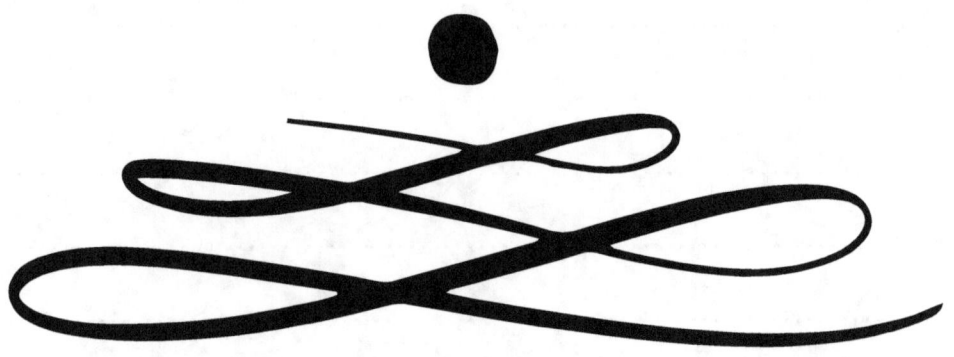

"The beginning is the most important part of the work..."

- Plato

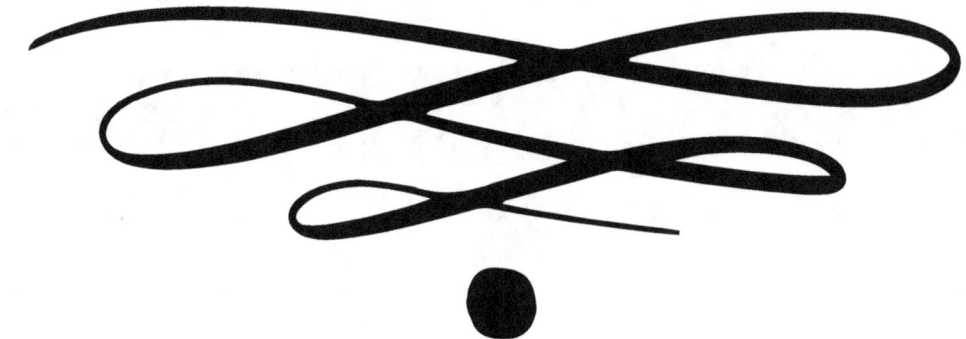

Writing Space

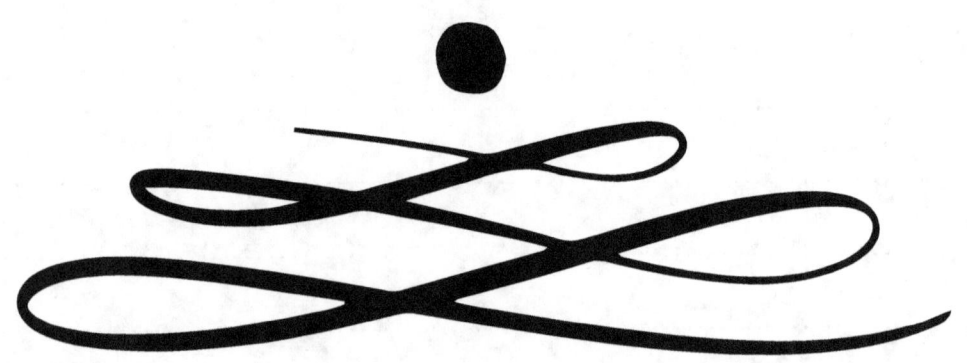

Write a poem about your favorite pastime.

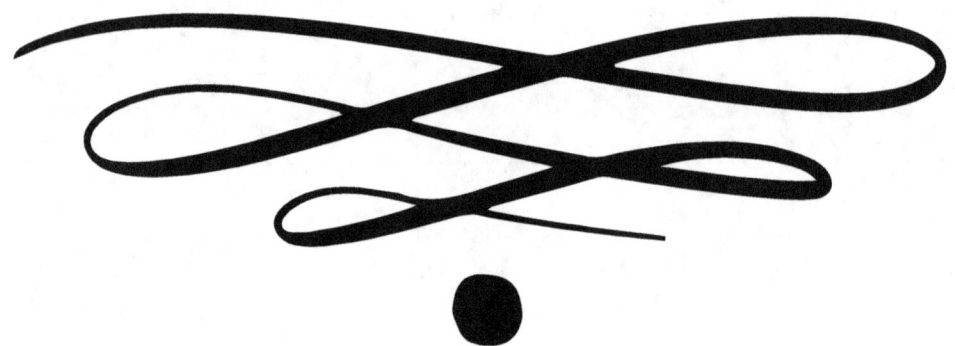

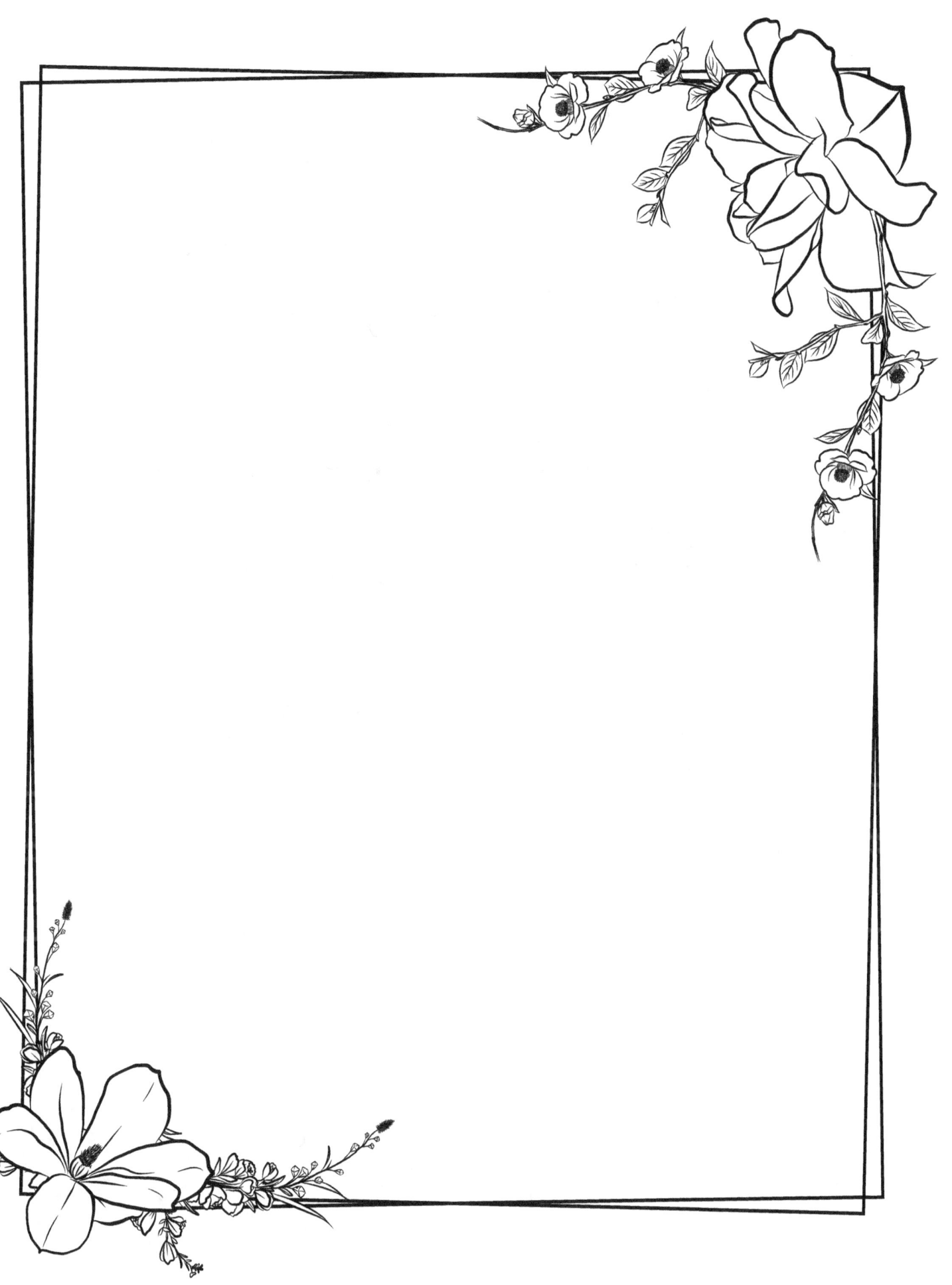

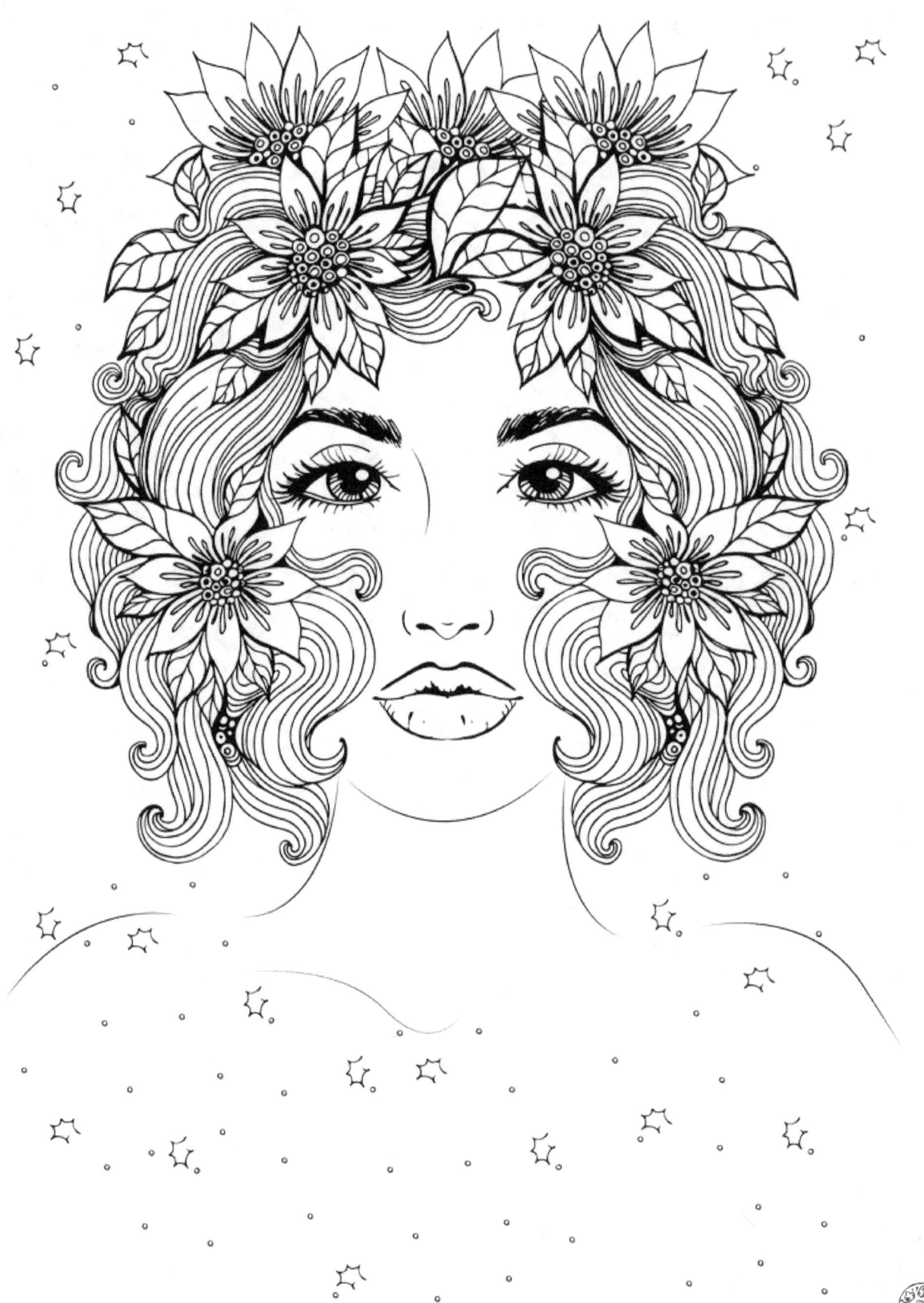

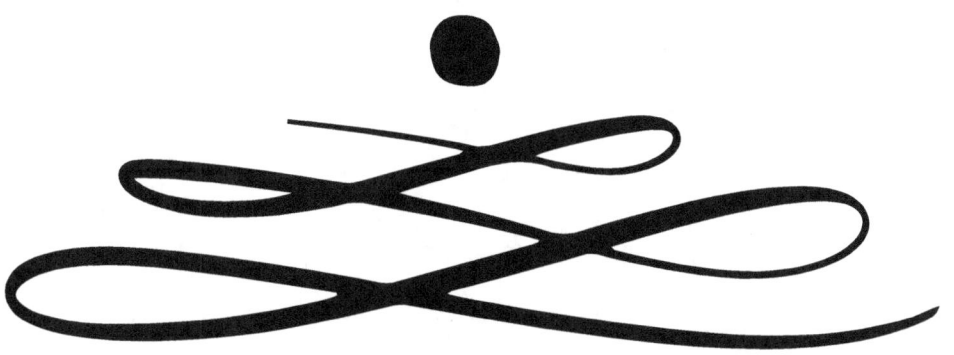

"Beware of missing chances; otherwise it may be altogether too late some day."

- Franz Liszt, Hungarian musician,
1811-1886

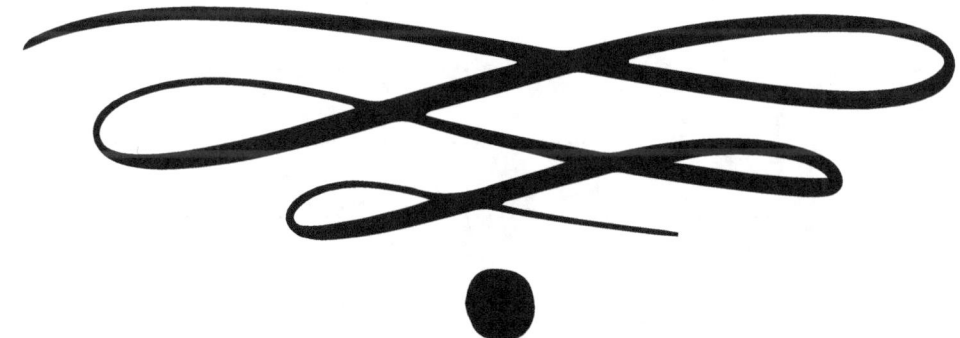

Writing Space

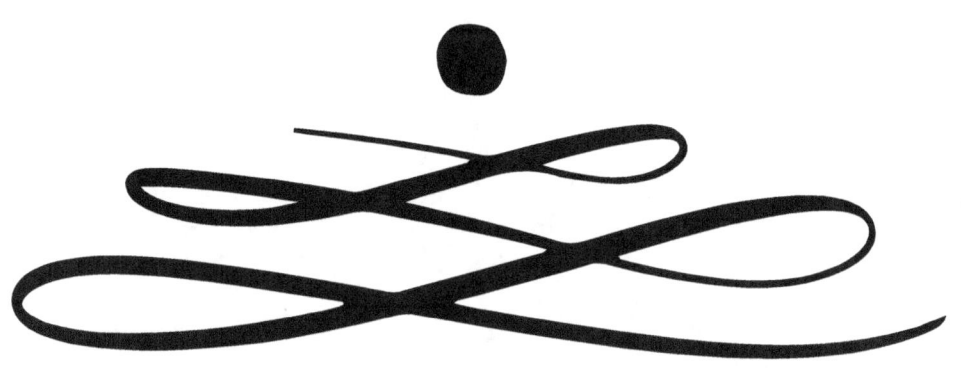

Write about your best year.

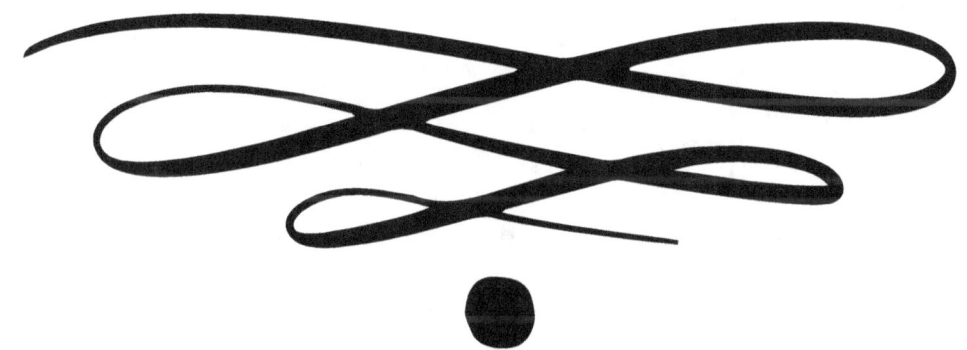

Writing Space

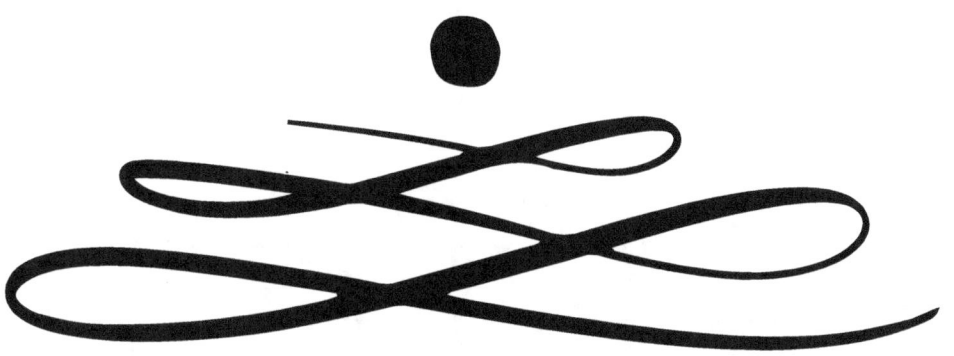

"The greatest test of courage on earth is to bear defeat without losing heart."

- Robert Green Ingersoll, American political leader, 1833-1899

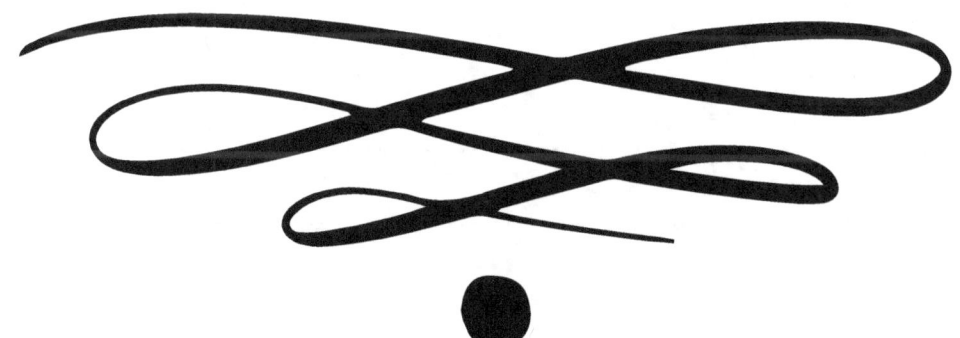

Writing Space

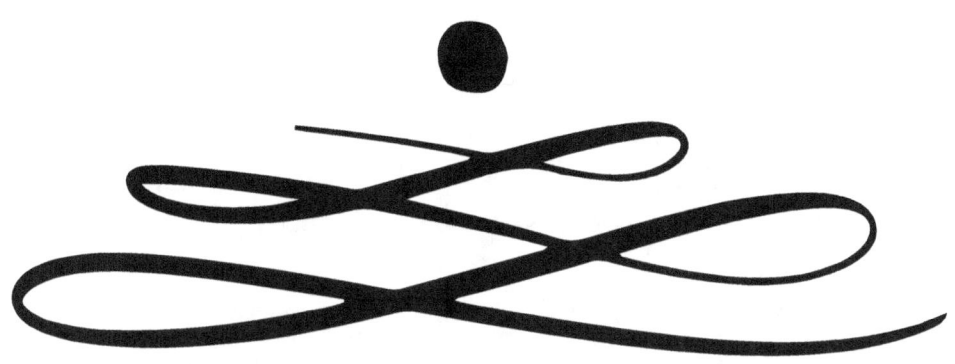

Write about a time when you changed your mind.

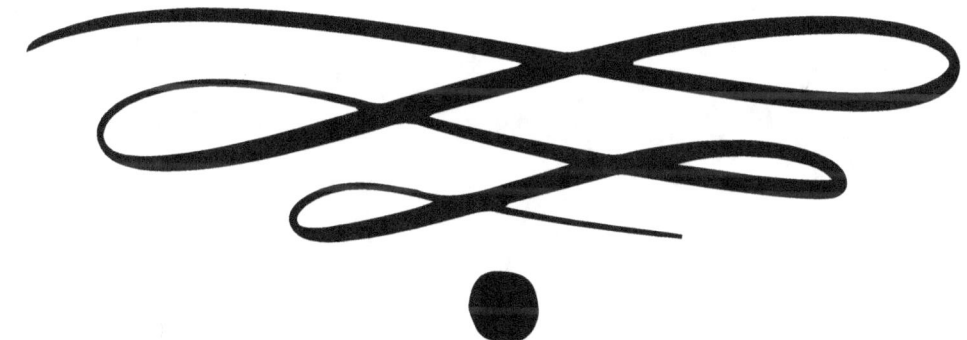

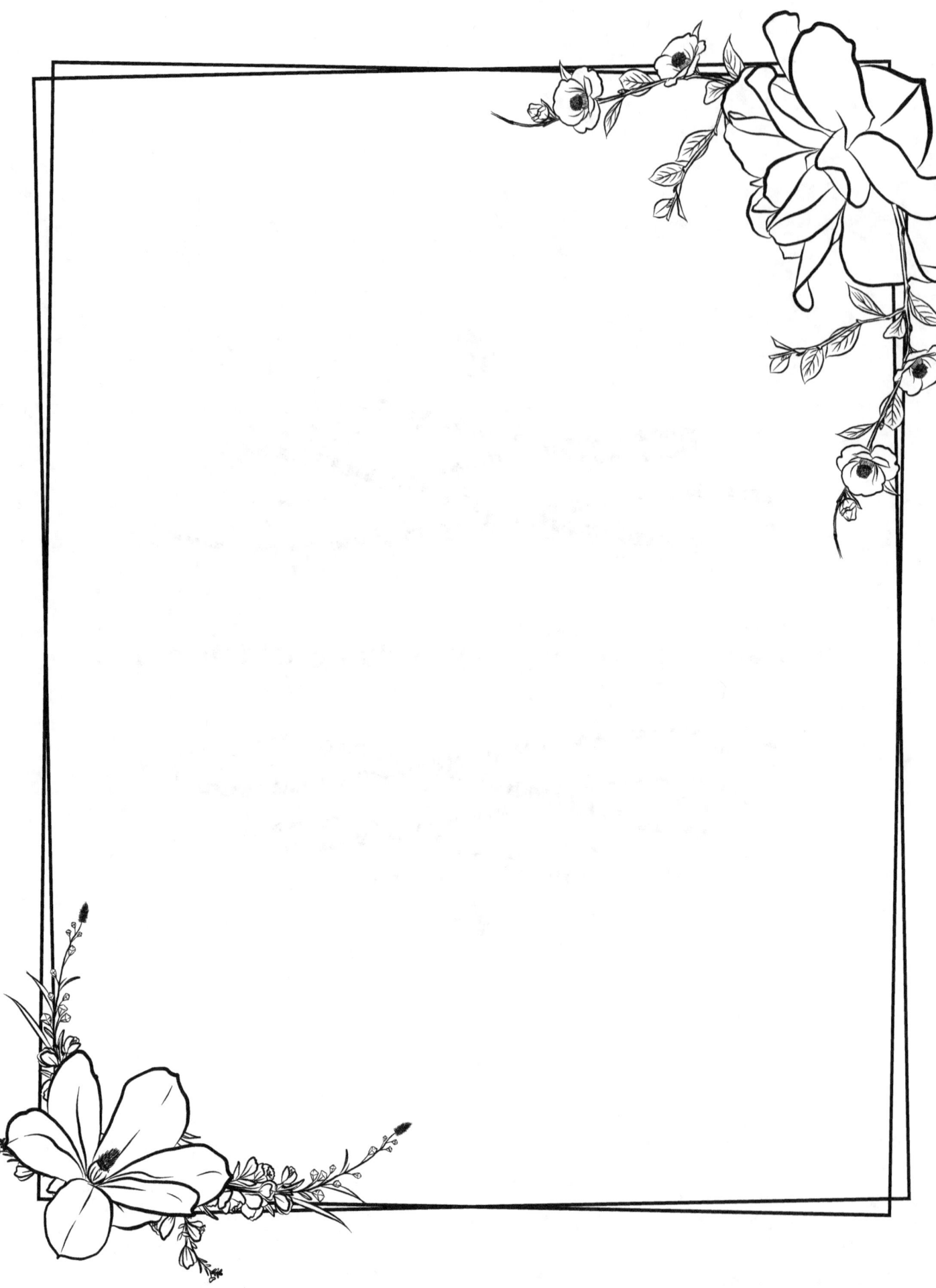

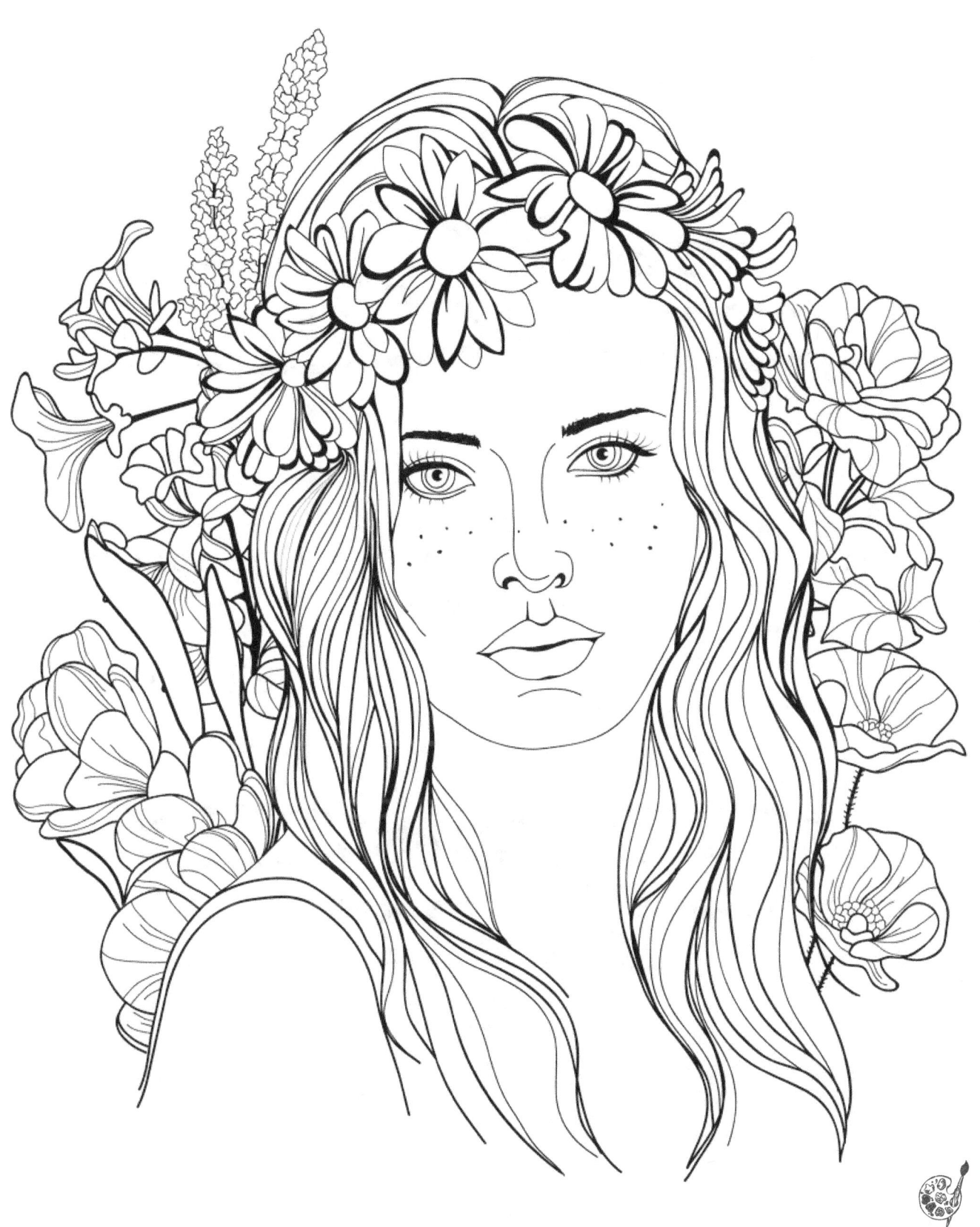

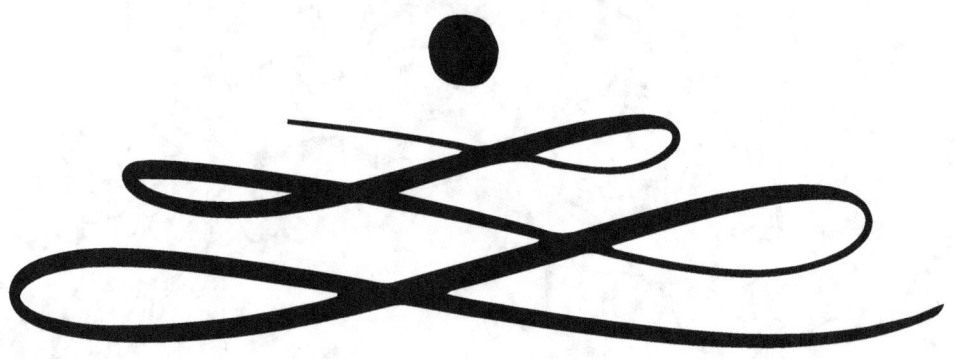

"Life is like a cup of tea, the sugar is all at the bottom!"

- Julia Ward Howe

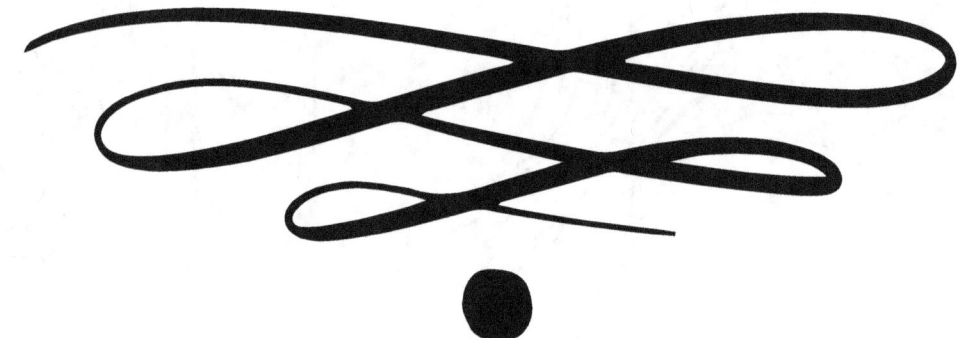

Writing Space

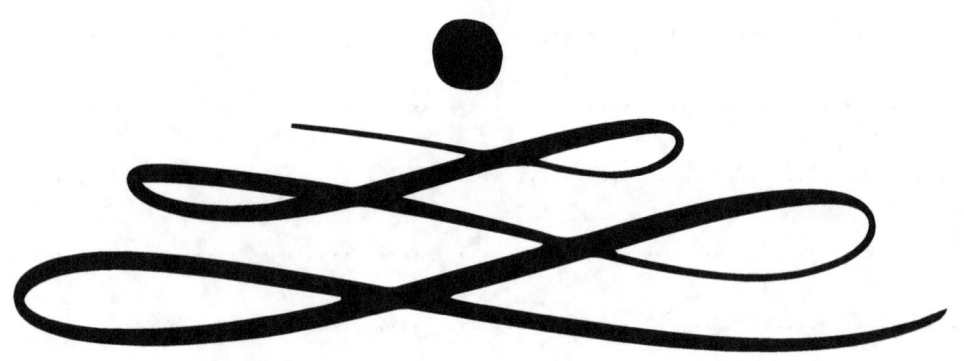

Write about a missed opportunity.

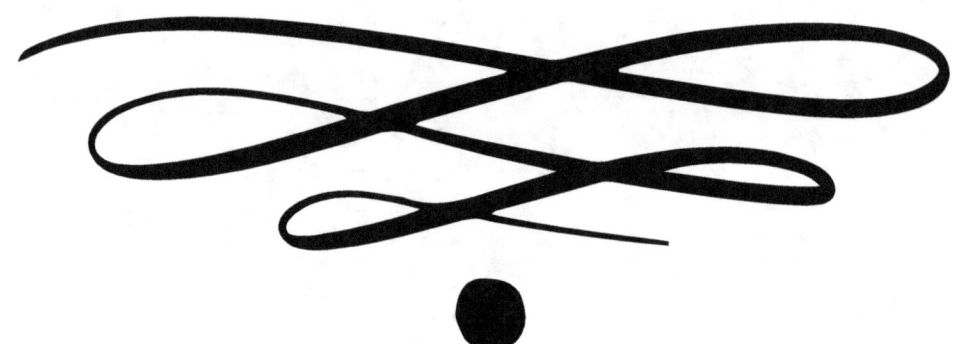

Writing Space

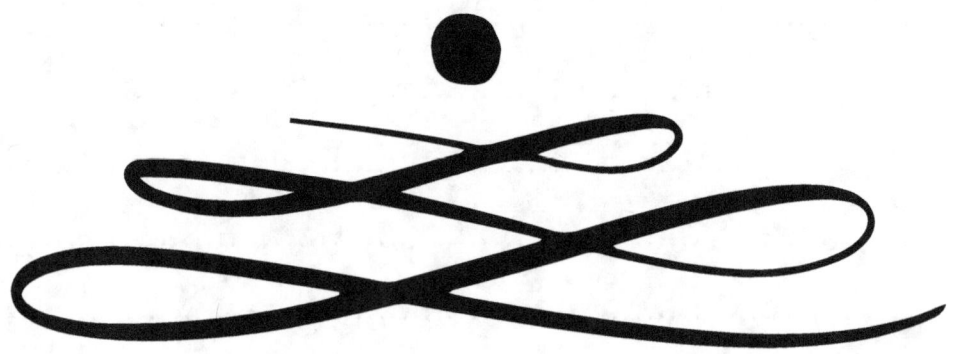

"Be less curious about people and more curious about ideas..."

- Marie Curie

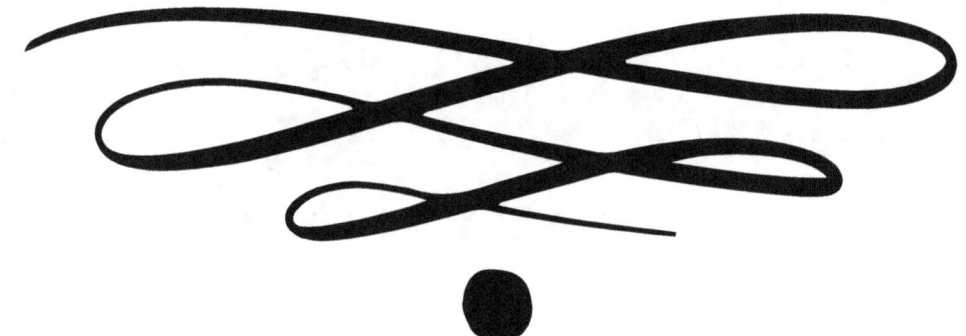

Writing Space

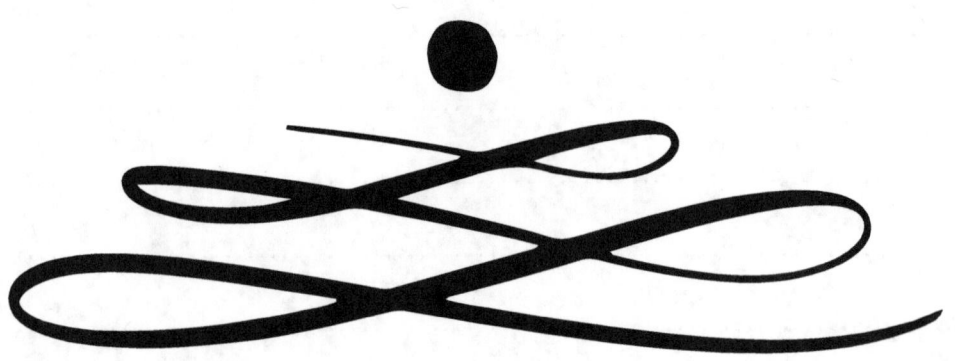

Imagine you got a chance to start over from scratch.

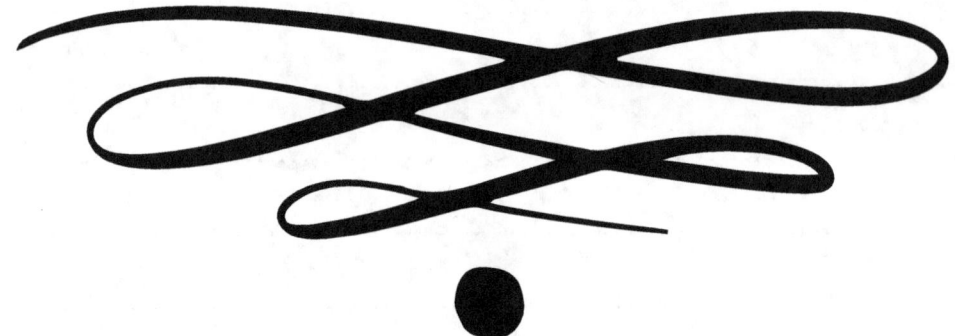

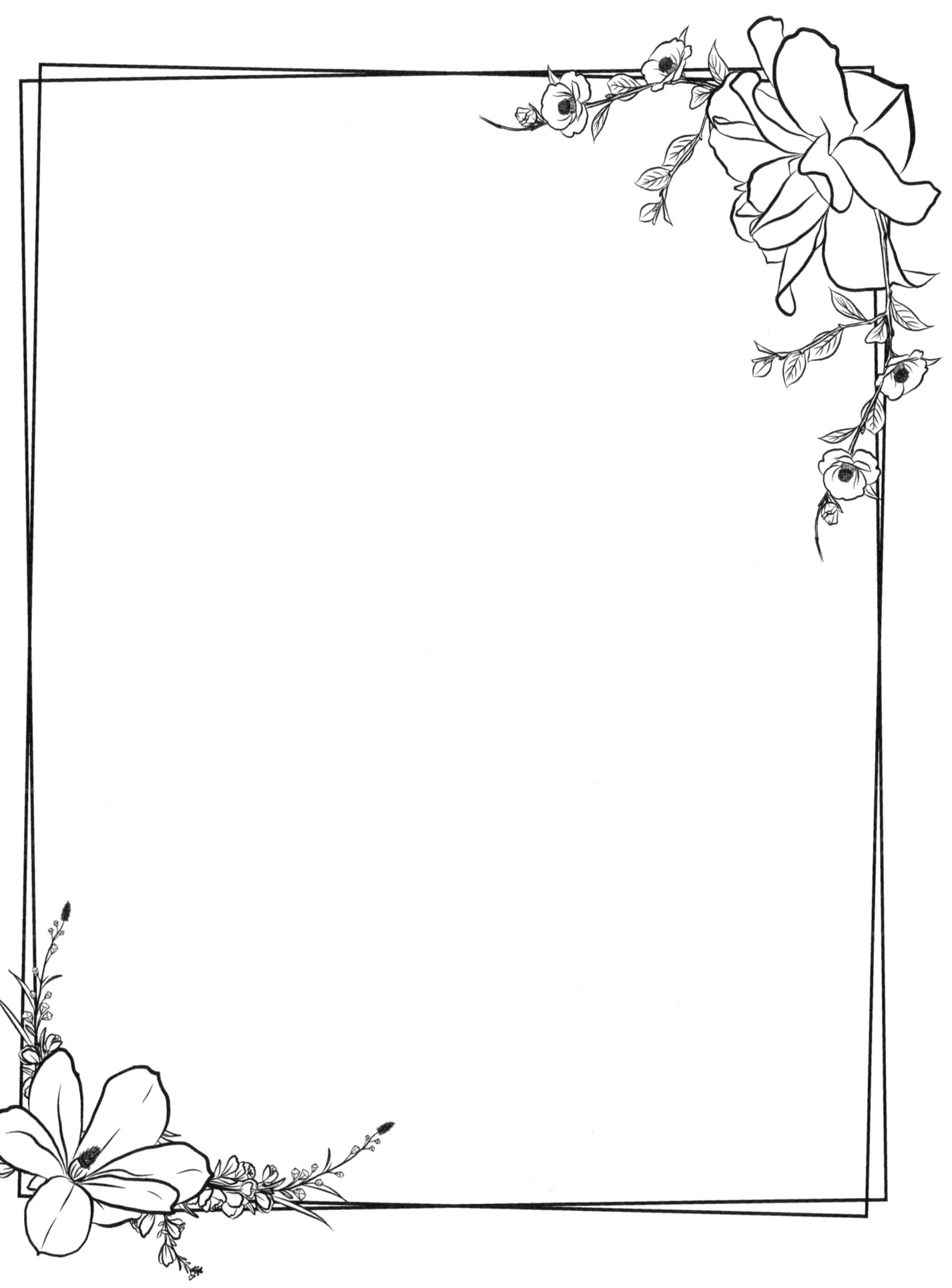

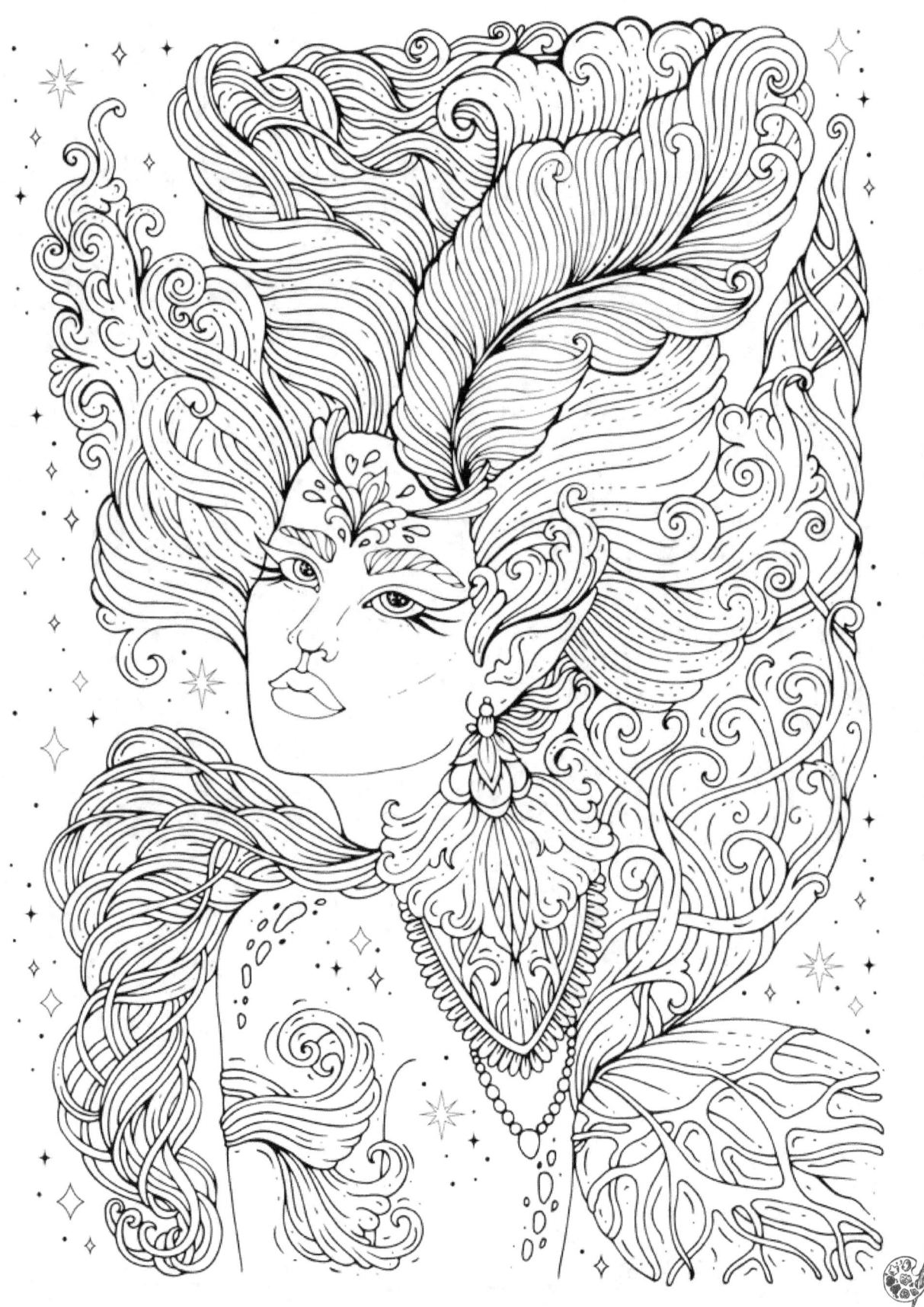

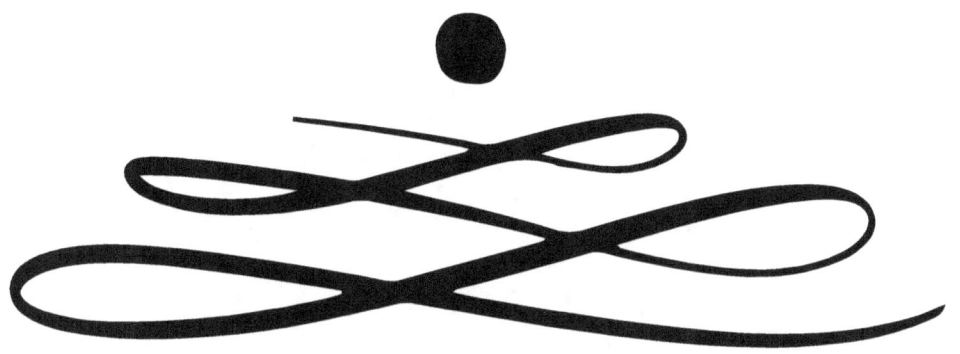

"Experience is the teacher of all things."

- Julius Caesar, Roman politician,
100-44 BC

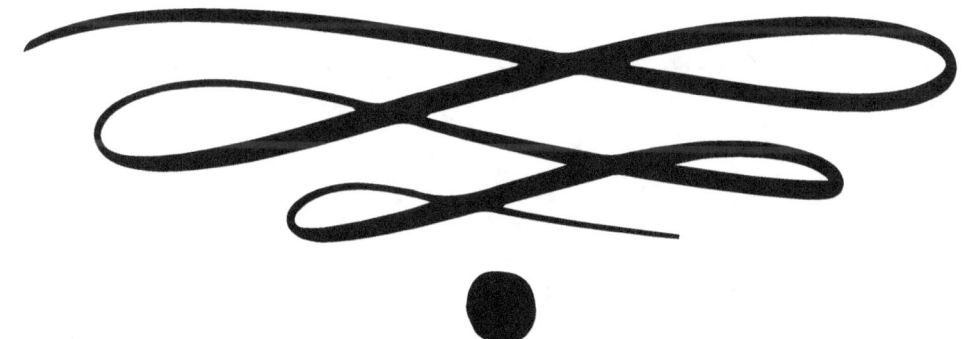

Writing Space

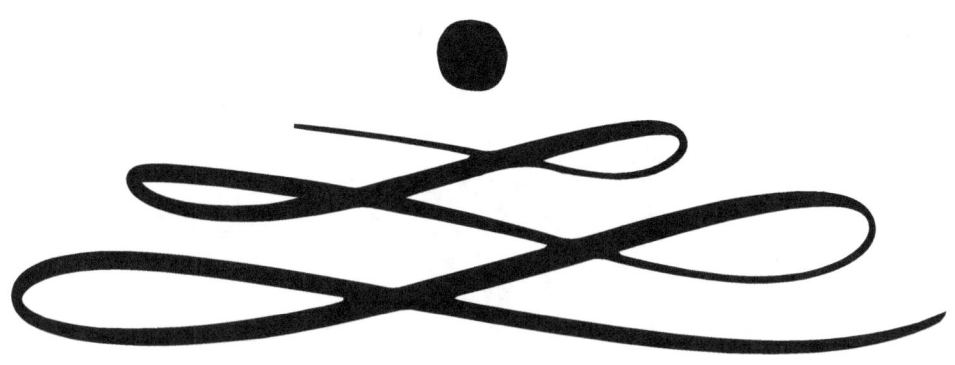

Write about a time your biggest mistake became your best opportunity.

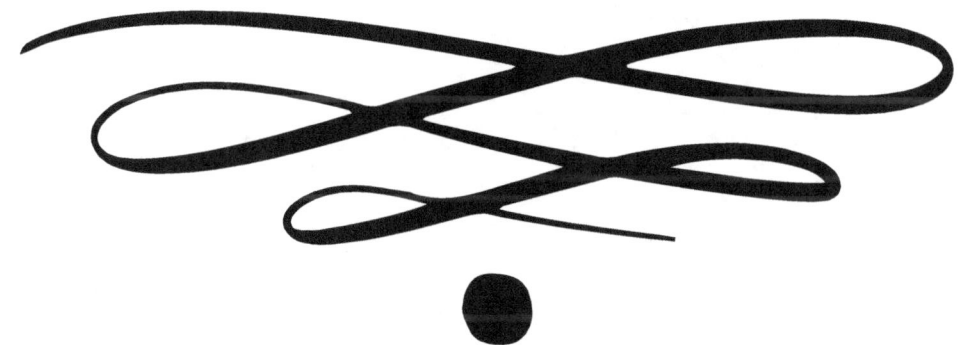

Writing Space

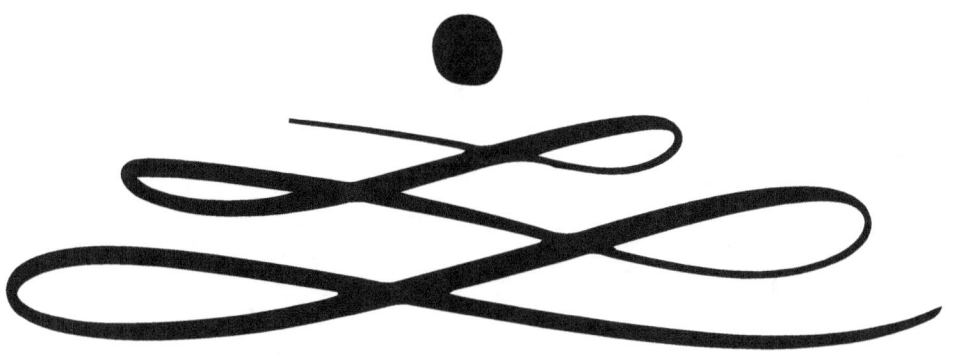

"My destination is no longer a place, rather a new way of seeing…"

- Marcel Proust

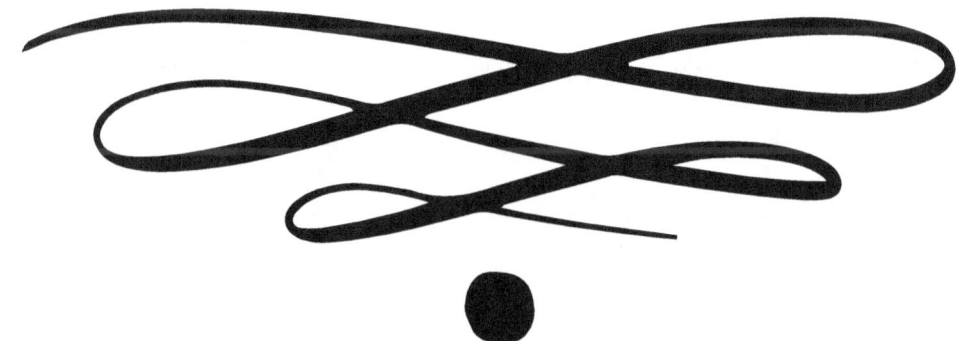

Writing Space

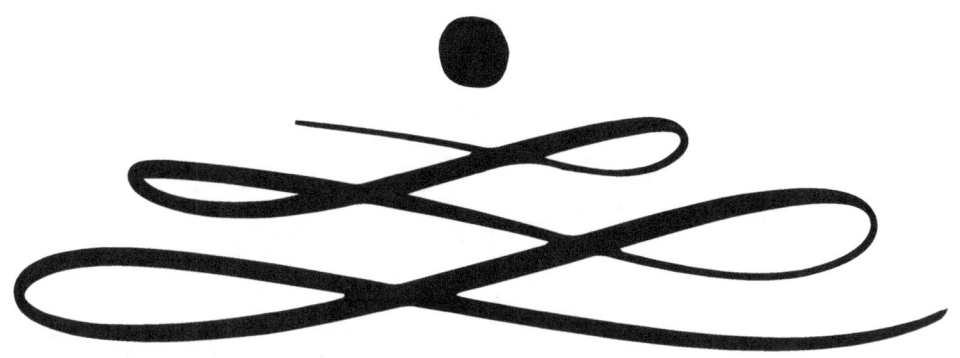

Write a poem about your favorite holiday.

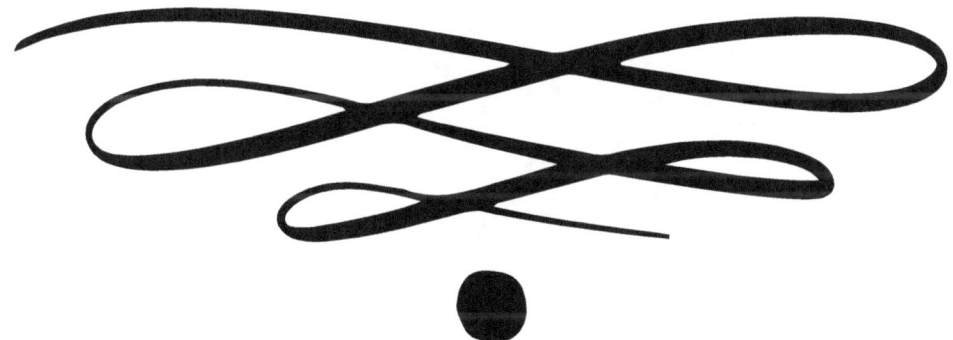

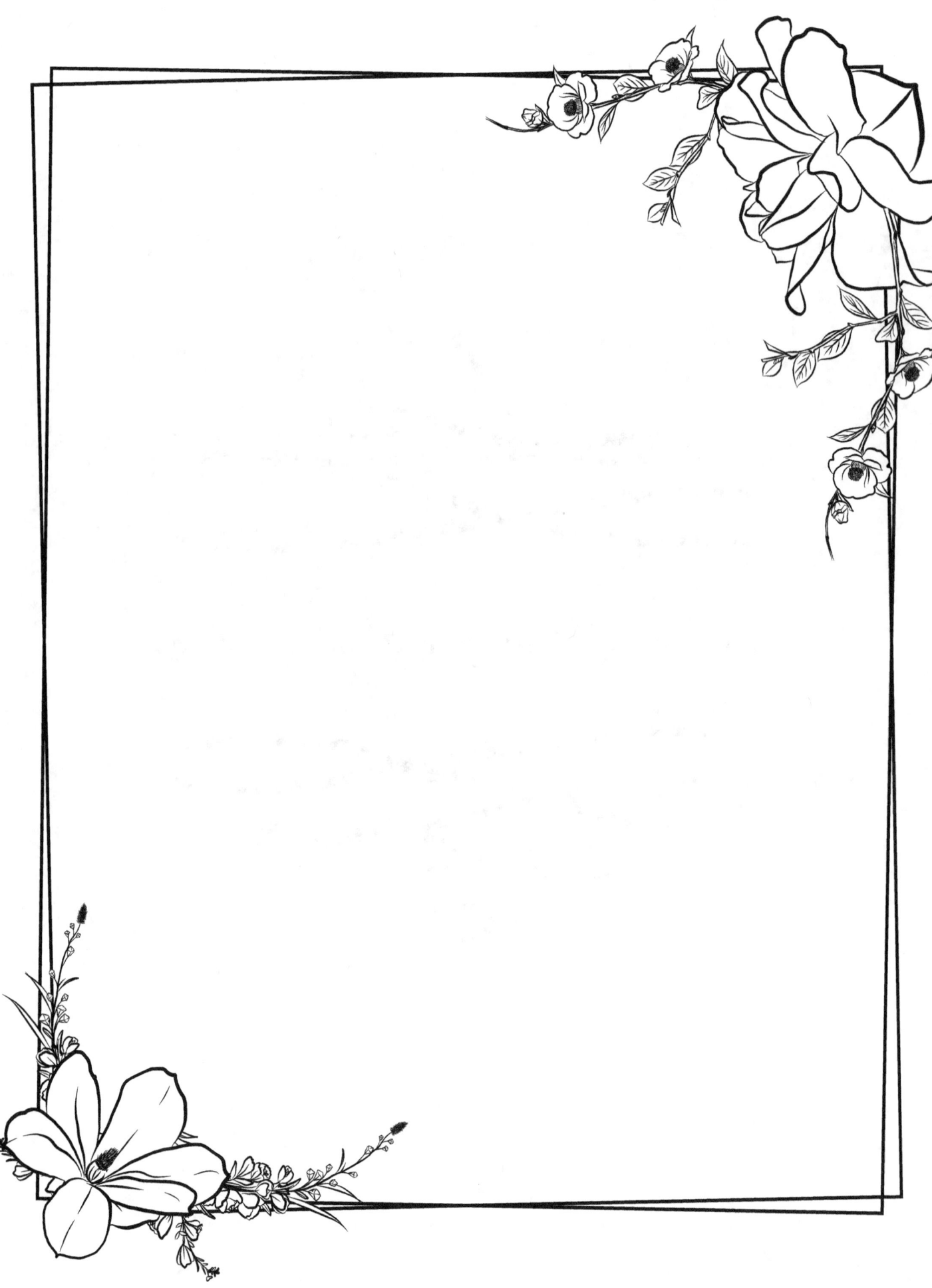

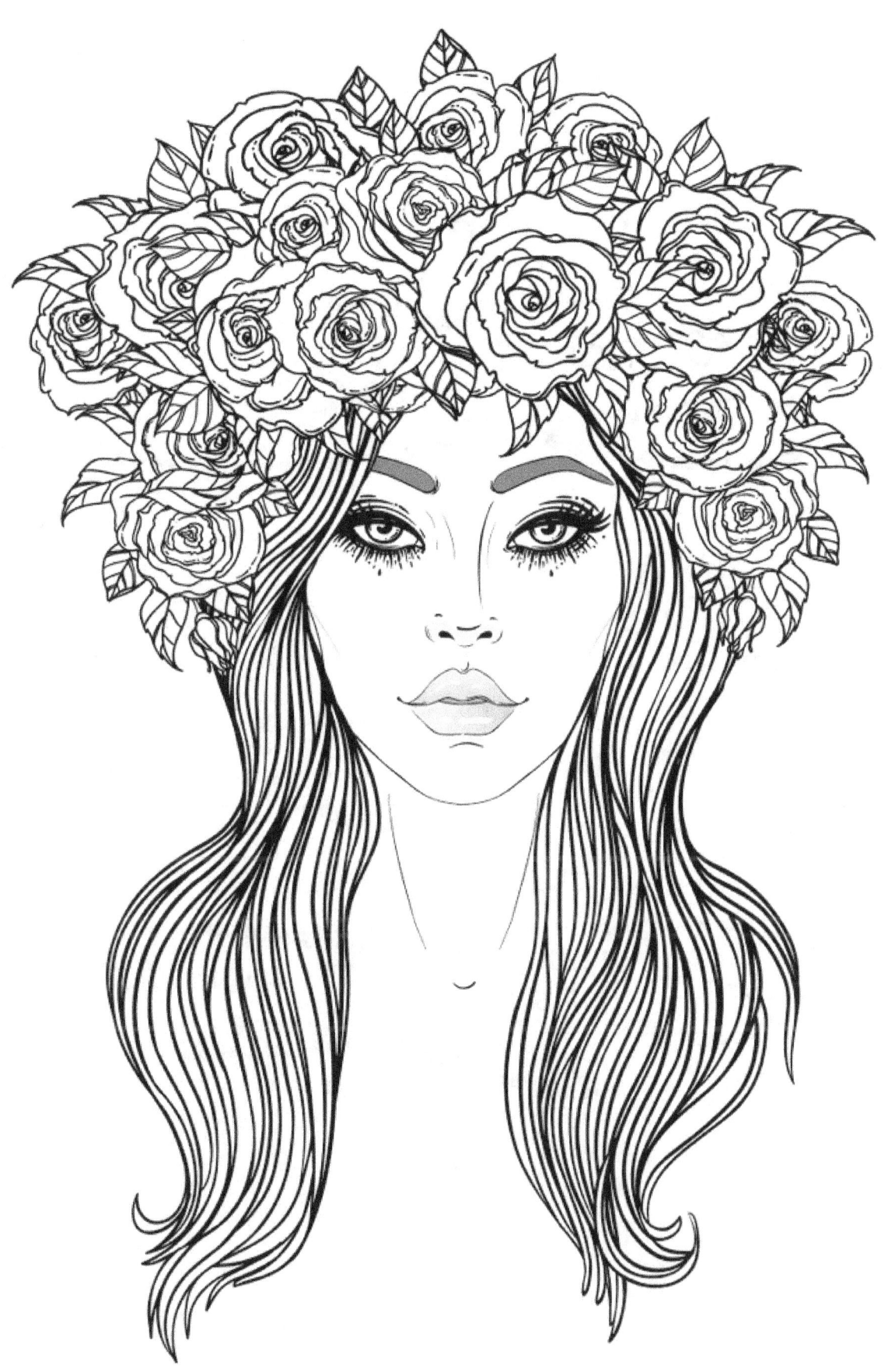

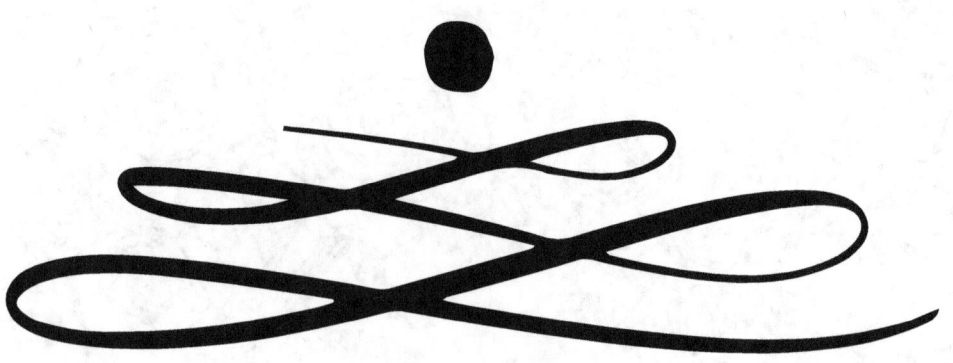

"The great aim of education is not knowledge but action."

Herbert Spencer, English philosopher, 1820-1903

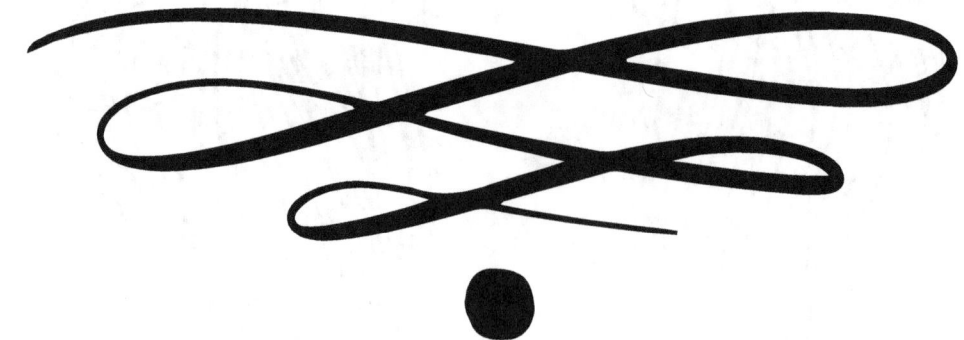

Writing Space

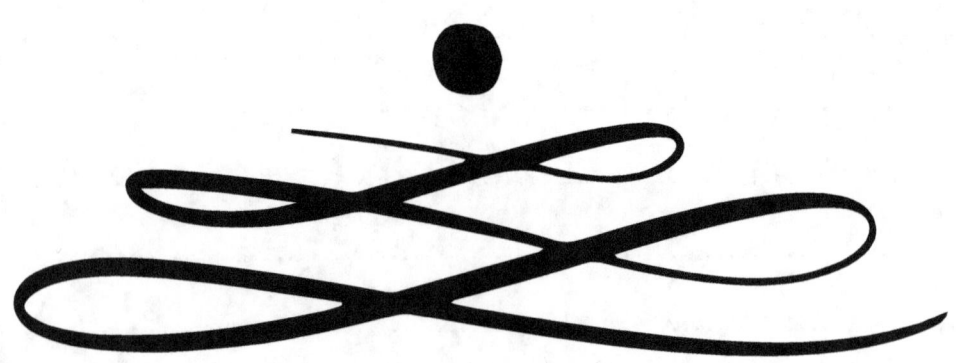

Write a poem about midnight.

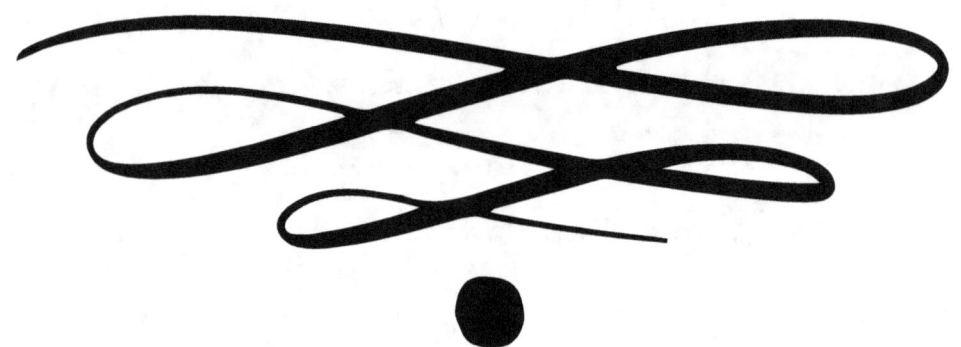

Writing Space

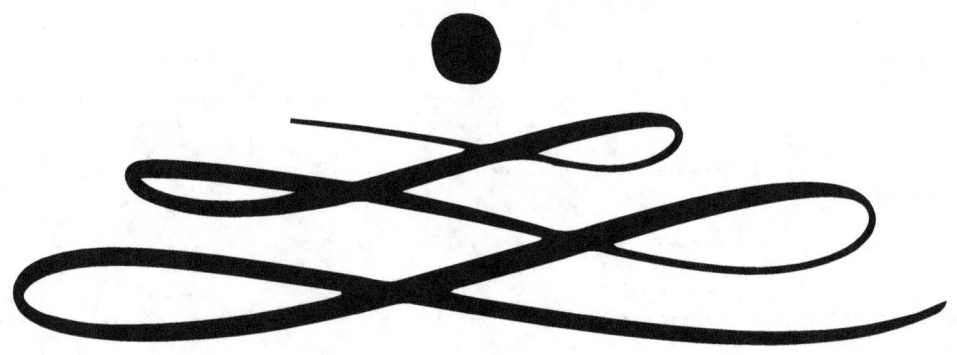

"It is the mark of an educated mind to be able to entertain a thought without accepting it."

- Aristotle, Ancient Greek philosopher

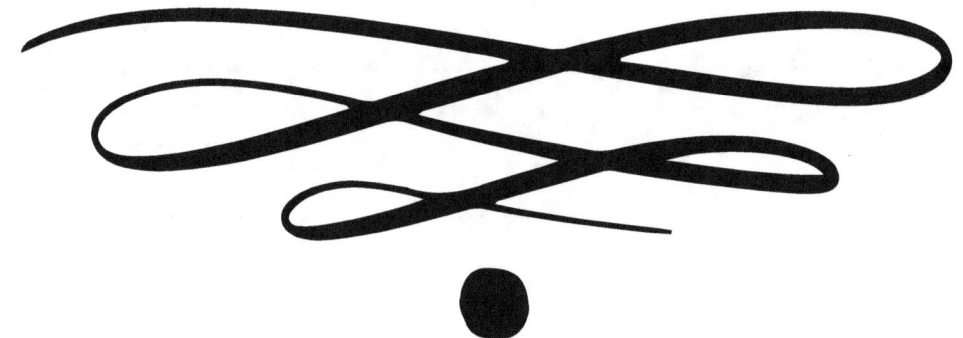

Writing Space

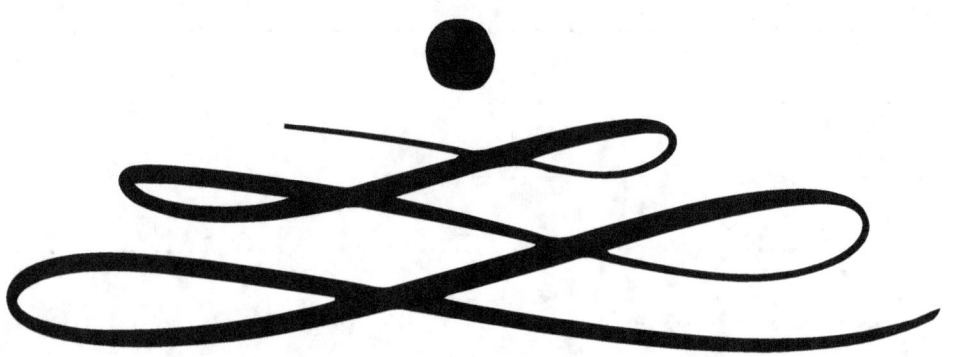

"Listen with ears of tolerance! See through the eyes of compassion! Speak with the language of love..."

- Rumi

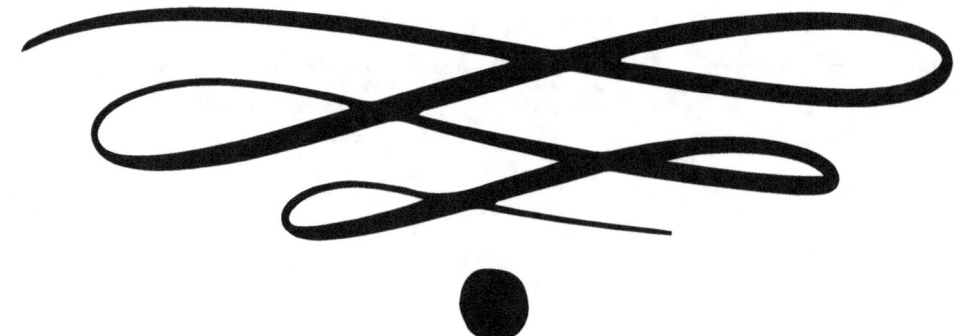

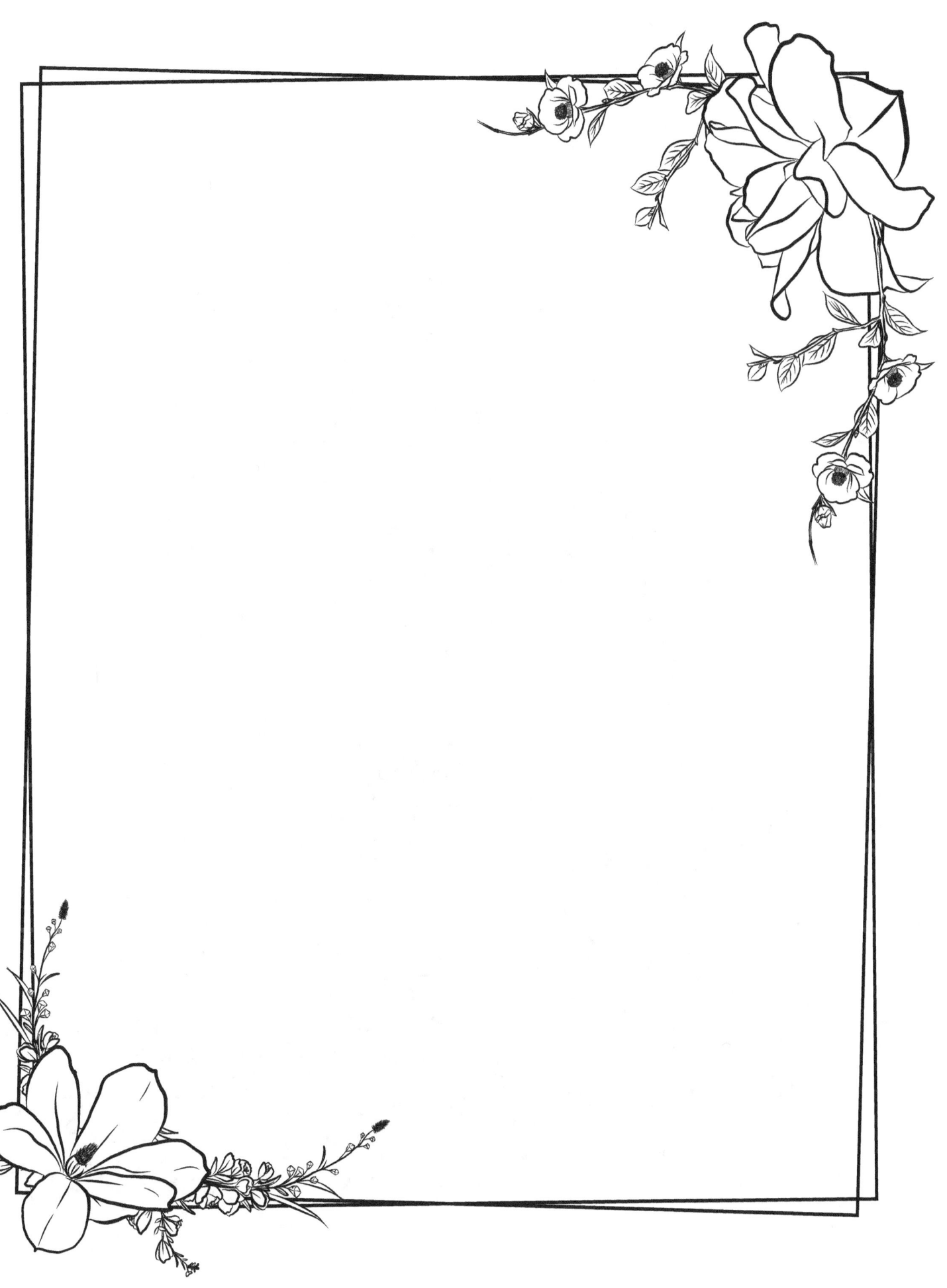

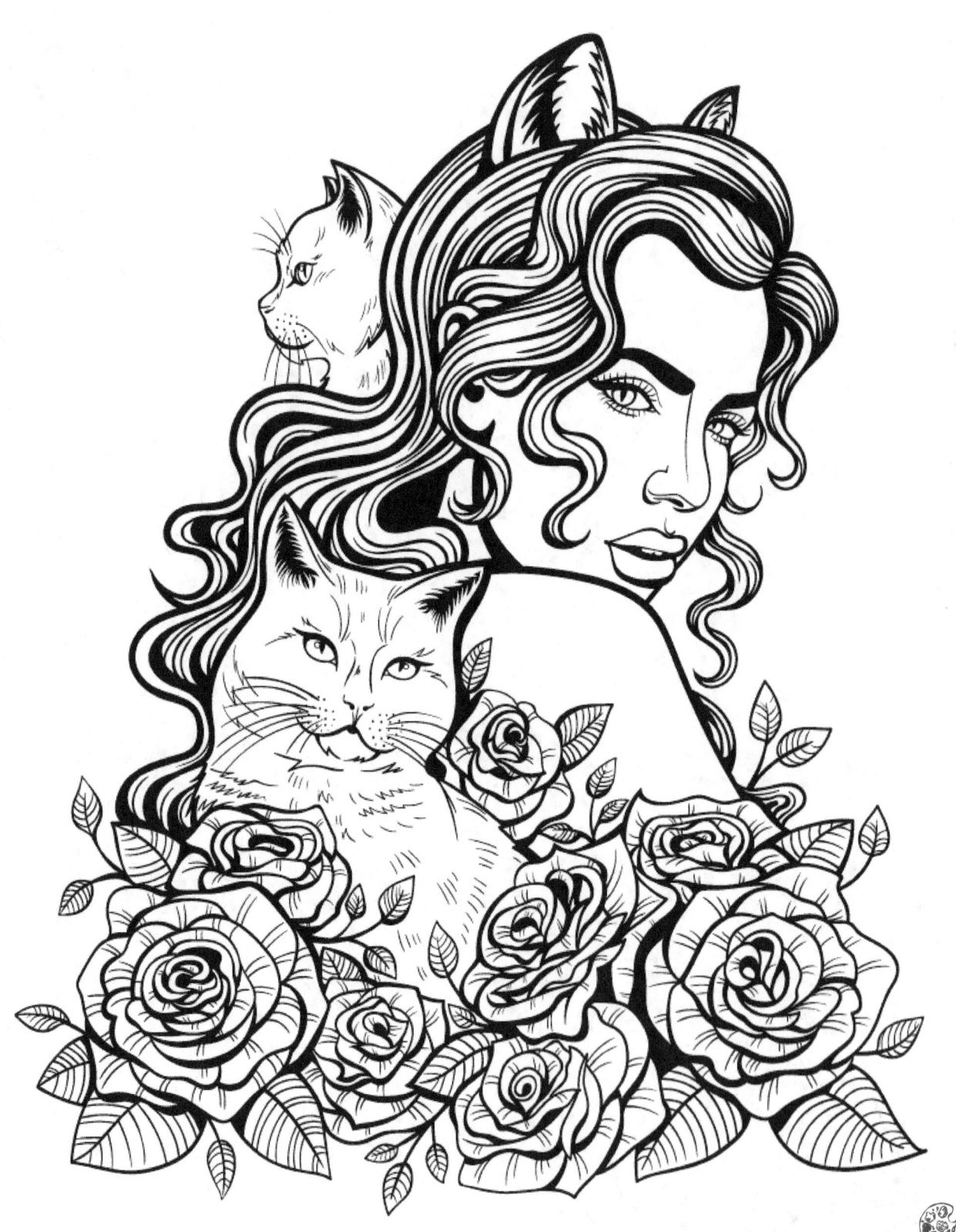

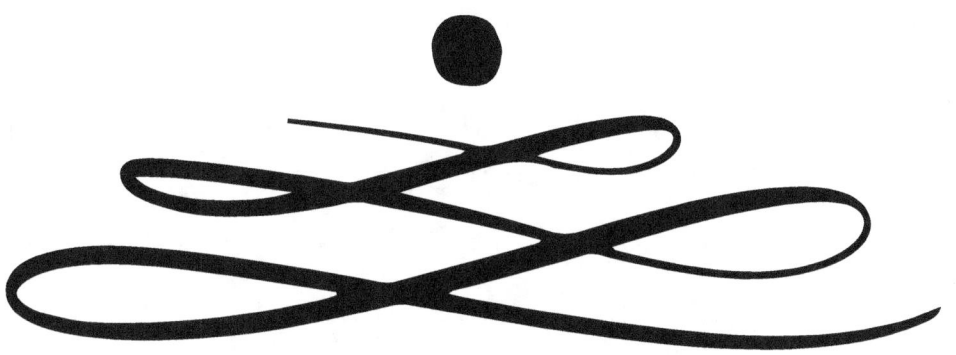

"It's amazing how lovely common things become, if one only knows how to look at them…"

- Louisa May Alcott

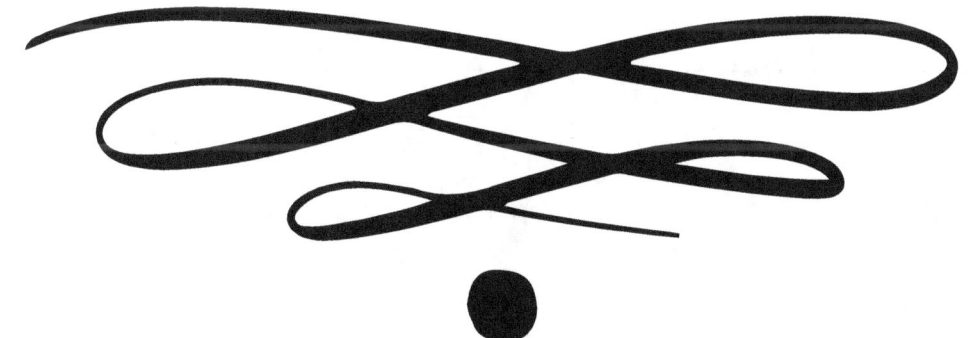

Writing Space

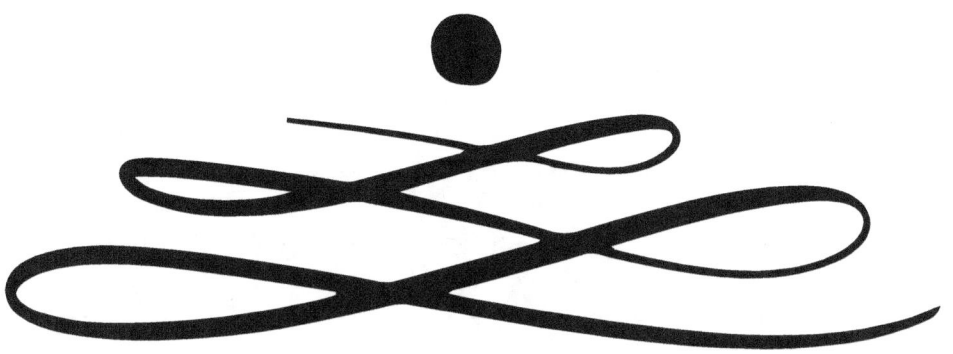

"What you want to ignite in others must first burn inside yourself..."

- Charlotte Bronte

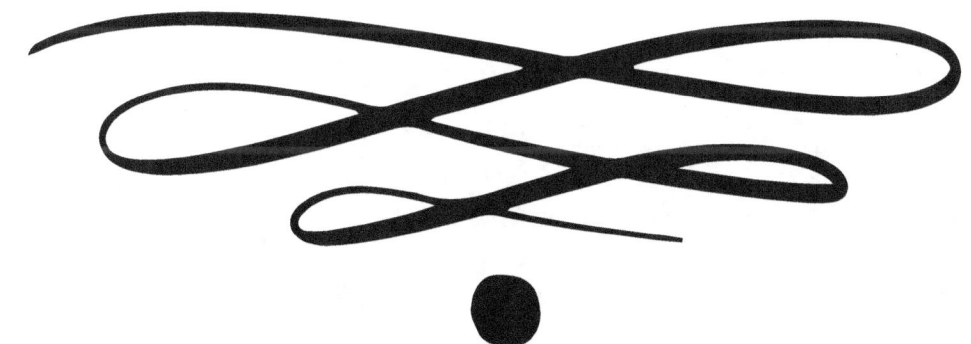

Writing Space

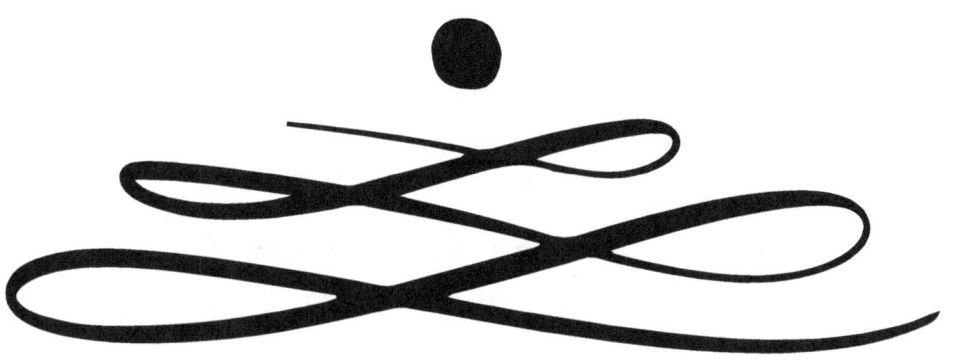

"Love is anterior to life, posterior to death, initial of creation, and the exponent of breath…"

- Emily Dickinson

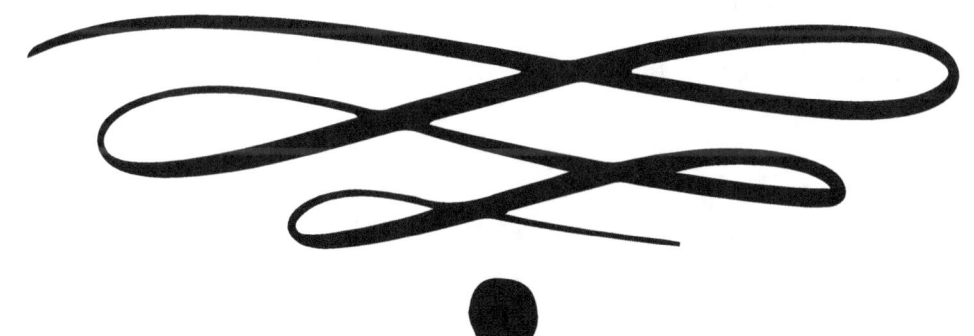

Writing Space

"Do not take life too seriously. You will never get out of it alive."

- Elbert Hubbard, American writer, 1859-1915

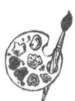

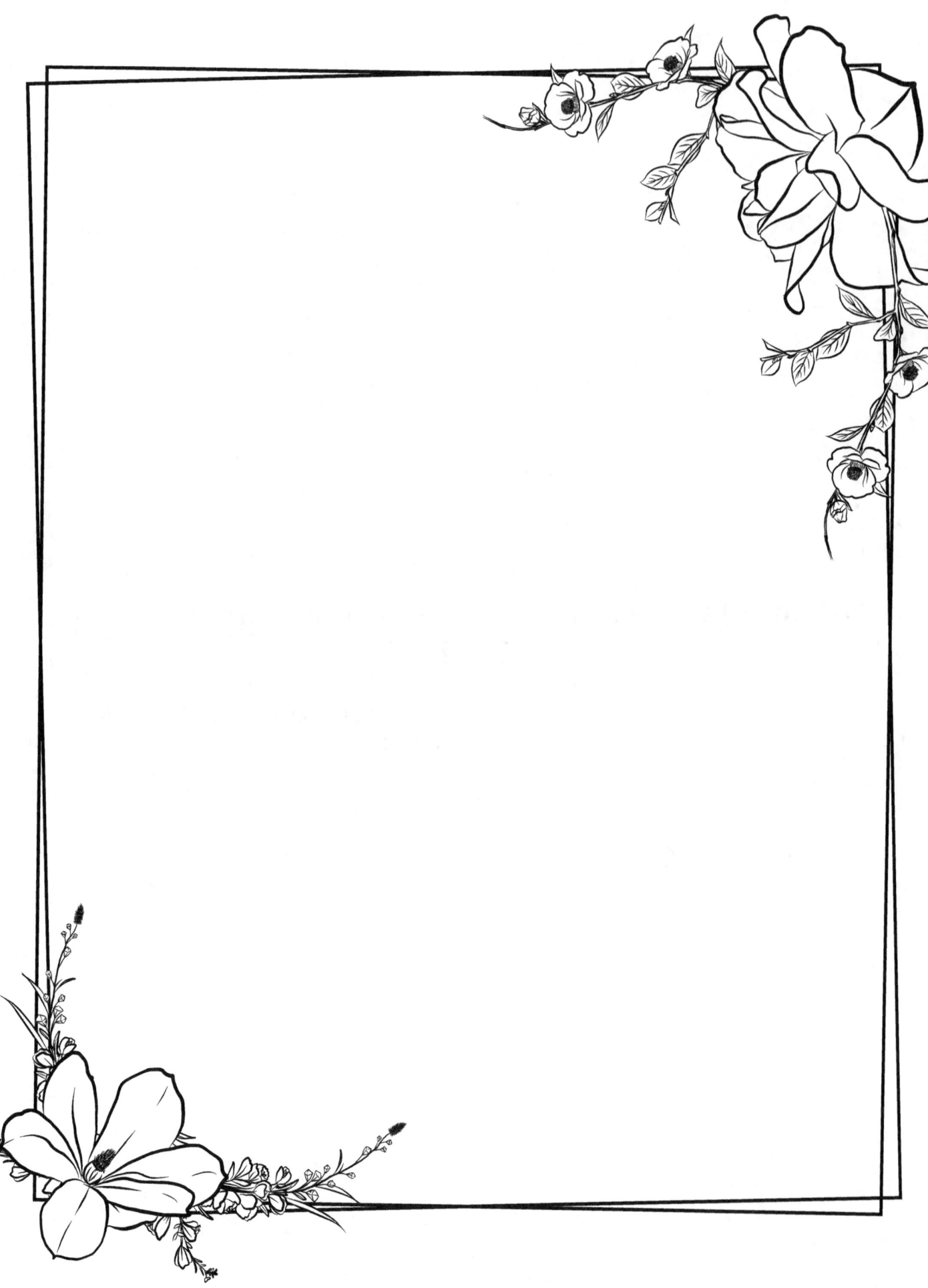